WIRED DIFFERENTLY

—

30 Neurodivergent People You Should Know

Joe Wells

Illustrated by Tim Stringer

Jessica Kingsley Publishers
London and Philadelphia

First published in Great Britain in 2022 by Jessica Kingsley Publishers
An imprint of Hodder & Stoughton Ltd
An Hachette Company

1

A CIP catalogue record for this title is available from the
British Library and the Library of Congress

ISBN 978 1 78775 842 1
eISBN 978 1 78775 843 8

Printed and bound in Great Britain by TJ Books Limited

Jessica Kingsley Publishers' policy is to use papers that are natural,
renewable and recyclable products and made from wood grown in
sustainable forests. The logging and manufacturing processes are expected
to conform to the environmental regulations of the country of origin.

Jessica Kingsley Publishers
Carmelite House
50 Victoria Embankment
London EC4Y 0DZ

www.jkp.com

MIX
Paper from
responsible sources
FSC® C013056

WIRED DIFFERENTLY

of related interest

Creative, Successful, Dyslexic
23 High Achievers Share Their Stories
Margaret Rooke
Foreword by Mollie King
ISBN 978 1 78592 060 8 (paperback)
ISBN 978 1 84905 653 3 (hardback)
eISBN 978 1 78450 163 1

**The Bigger Picture Book of Amazing
Dyslexics and the Jobs They Do**
Kathy Iwanczak Forsyth and Kate Power
Foreword by Paul Smith
ISBN 978 1 78592 584 9
eISBN 978 1 78592 585 6

Different Like Me
My Book of Autism Heroes
Jennifer Elder
Illustrated by Marc Thomas and Jennifer Elder
ISBN 978 1 84310 815 3
eISBN 978 1 84642 466 3

ADHD Is Our Superpower
The Amazing Talents and Skills of Children with ADHD
Soli Lazarus
Illustrated by Adriana Camargo
ISBN 978 1 78775 730 1
eISBN 978 1 78775 731 8

Gender Pioneers
A Celebration of Transgender,
Non-Binary and Intersex Icons
Philippa Punchard
Foreword by Christine Burns
ISBN 978 1 78775 515 4
eISBN 978 1 78775 514 7

For Danika

Contents

Welcome

p.9

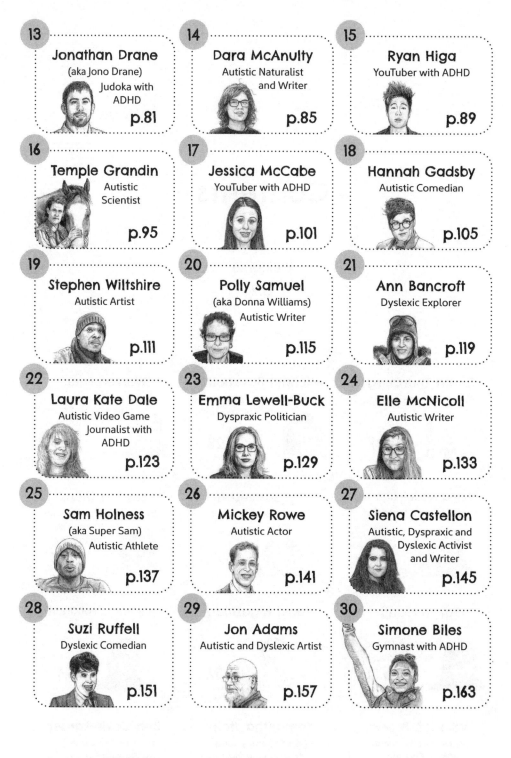

WELCOME

No one in this book is normal. They're all very unusual and that's why I've written about them. I've got nothing against 'normal' people but, with respect to all the normal people out there, they tend not to be worth writing about. I want to write about the unusual people, who come up with strange ideas, know loads about one particular thing or ask questions that no one else would think to ask.

There are so many people in the world – I've met thousands of them. A lot of them are pretty similar, but still, from time to time, I will meet someone who isn't like anyone else, and that is the greatest thrill in the world. I'll think that there must be only a certain number of ways to be a human, but then someone new and completely unique will come along and I'll think, 'Wow! You've put a whole new spin on what it means to be a human, like when Pizza Hut brought out that pizza which had little cheeseburgers in the crust!'

I was unusual when I was growing up. I was called weird by the other kids at school (and the occasional teacher). They were right. I am weird; I don't like making eye contact, I sometimes ask people questions they don't like and I can talk about hip-hop music for longer than most people can talk at all. My brain is the main part of me that is unusual (although I do have one toe which is much longer than the others). My mum used to say that I was 'wired differently'. I like the term 'wired differently'; it makes me think that all our brains are computers and that mine is set up for specialist programs that would crash most computers.

When I was at school, I felt like I had to hide my differently wired brain so that I fitted in, which seems ridiculous now. Now I wouldn't want to be anything other than differently wired because most of my favourite people are that way, too.

At school, I didn't really know any other people with brains like mine. The other kids all seemed to have 'normal' brains (looking back, this can't have been true) and everything was set up for how their brains worked. This meant all the kids with 'normal' brains got to show off what they could do with their brains, and the things I could do with my differently wired brain weren't seen as that important. If your brain is wired differently, and you're expected to be like people with 'normal' brains, it can sometimes feel like your brain is wired wrong – but it isn't!

I spent a lot of time when I was younger trying to behave more like a 'normal' brained person (this is sometimes called 'masking'), but as I got older, I started to meet other people with differently wired brains and I liked them a lot more than the 'normal' people I knew. Some of those people are in this book, and some of them have diagnoses like autism, dyspraxia, dyslexia and ADHD.

When I was 29, I received a diagnosis of autism, but I've since felt conflicted about it. It seems odd to me that we use the same type of language to describe differently wired brains as we use to describe horrible diseases.

Welcome

'This person has a diagnosis of autism.'

'Oh no! Can it be cured? Will it get worse? Is it contagious?'

I think this is why a lot of autistic people prefer to be called 'autistic people', rather than 'people with autism'. 'Joe is autistic' sounds like it's part of who I am; 'Joe has autism' sounds like I'm carrying it around with me.

My friend taught me about a thing called *neurodiversity*. It's sort of three things really – it's a fact, a belief and a movement to change the world.

The fact of neurodiversity is that, in human society, everyone's brain is different. In the same way that humans have different hair, different eyes and different taste in hats, we all have a different brain. This is just a fact – you can go to any public place and you will find that different people have different brains.

Neurodiversity is also a belief. It's the belief that us all having different brains is a good thing. For this reason, people who believe in neurodiversity don't try to change or fix people whose brains are different – we think difference is good.

OK, before I go any further, let me equip you with some of the language that I'll be using in this book. The people who have the most 'normal' types of brains, I'll be calling 'neurotypical', and the people who have differently wired brains, I'll refer to as 'neurodivergent'. When I talk about a group of people with different brains, I'll use the term 'neurodiverse'. On the next page is a little cut-out-and-keep glossary which you may find helpful.

Cut-out-and-keep glossary

Neurodiversity – this term refers to the fact that human brains are different, the belief that this is a good thing and the movement to create a world where all brains are included and get to reach their full potential.

Neurodiverse – this describes a group of people who have different brains. For example, 'this college class has a neurodiverse group of students'.

Neurodivergent – this describes people whose brains are different to the majority of people's brains. This includes people with dyspraxia, dyslexia, autism, ADHD and some people who don't fit neatly into one diagnosis.

Neurotypical – this describes people with 'normal' brains which work in the way that society expects. It's the opposite of neurodivergent. It's estimated that in an average group of seven people, six will be neurotypical and one will be neurodivergent.

Where it gets complicated is that outside of this book you'll often find people using the word 'neurodiverse' to describe neuro*divergent* people. For example, 'this person is autistic, they are neurodiverse'. It doesn't really make sense to me: a person can't be neurodiverse for the same reason a cat can't be biodiverse (unless it has fleas, I suppose), but that's how people often use the term 'neurodiverse'. I think eventually everyone will catch up and realize that I was right and 'neurodivergent' is the correct term for people with differently wired brains, but for the time being we're going to have to deal with the confusion. When I see people using these terms incorrectly in other books, I get a pen, cross out the word 'neurodiverse' and write 'neurodivergent' underneath. You're welcome to do the same, but don't blame me if you get thrown out of the library.

Neurodiversity is also the belief that there are limitations to the ways that we categorize neurodivergent brains. When we diagnose people, we tend to lump them into groups, but the people within those groups can be completely different from each other. There are also some people with differently wired brains who don't fit neatly into one diagnosis. I like this about neurodiversity – there's no one at the door saying, 'Sorry, we can't find the right label for you. You can't come in.'

I believe that neurodiversity is one of the most important ideas people are talking about today and it will change the world for the better. It's a fairly new idea, and a lot of people haven't quite bought into it yet, but I think it will follow the same path as other once radical ideas like evolution, gravity or Netflix. It will take some time, but sooner or later it's really going to catch on.

It's not that radical when you think about it. Lots of other things in nature are diverse and better for it, so why shouldn't our brains be diverse too? Seeing neurodivergent brains as broken or diseased is like saying that cats are a type of broken dog – they aren't broken, they're just different. And just as our ecosystems need different animals doing different things, our human societies need all sorts of different people being teachers and scientists and artists and electricians and whatever a podiatrist does (it's either feet or spines – I get it mixed up).

So why are so many people not yet sold on this idea? We still refer to ways of being neurodivergent as conditions which people 'suffer' from, we still see articles in the news where parents refer to 'grieving' for their (still alive) neurodivergent child, and the autism 'treatment' industry in America alone is estimated to be worth 1.8 billion dollars (for comparison, Jay-Z is worth 1 billion dollars).

Our schools don't always help to promote the benefits of neurodiversity. Neurodiversity wants to celebrate everyone being different and having different strengths and weaknesses, whereas schools too often focus on training you up to be one type of person (which usually means a neurotypical person).

That leads me on to the final definition of neurodiversity. It's a movement! A really exciting and radical one, which wants to completely change how the world works so that neurodivergent people get properly included and valued. I've included some people in this book who are active parts of this movement such as Lydia X.Z. Brown and Jessica Thom. I hope that this book inspires you to join us, get stuck in and change the world.

There's a quote people attribute to Albert Einstein which is something like 'if we judge a fish by its ability to climb a tree, then it will live its whole life believing it is stupid'. There's actually no evidence that Einstein ever said this, and I've said it now so I'm claiming it as my quote. What this quote means (and I should know because I came up with it) is that some great people can be made to feel like failures because they're being judged on things they're not good at. If they had a chance to excel at the things that they *are* good at, then everyone would see how brilliant they are.

That's what all of the people in this book have in common. They have had a chance to show how brilliant they are and have done so proving why neurodiversity is good. The things they've achieved, created and inspired they did not *despite* being different but *because* they are different.

That's the most important idea in this book, so I'll say it again in case you missed it. These people haven't achieved *despite* being different; they've achieved *because* they are different. Remember that when reading this book. Say it out loud every time you turn the page, write it on a bit of paper to use as a bookmark – maybe even get it tattooed on the back of your hand? So many stories in the media talk about people 'overcoming' neurodivergent conditions in order to achieve something. The people in this book haven't done that. What they've overcome is an environment where all too often neurodivergent people don't get a fair chance. They are bulldozing a new path for future generations of neurodivergent people.

Everyone's welcome to read this book. If you're a neurotypical person reading it, then I hope it motivates you to play a role in creating those 'right circumstances' where being different can be a superpower. For every person in this book, there are dozens of other neurodivergent people who don't get to reach their potential.

We need you neurotypicals to help us to create more stories like the ones in this book.

If you're a neurodivergent person reading this, then I hope it welcomes you to the club. These people are unique, just like us! You'll probably have grown up hearing messages about how being different is a problem that needs to be fixed and you're probably going to hear those messages in the future, but difference is brilliant and important. The people in this book will have been told that their difference is a problem too, but they've not listened; they've leant into their difference and have been proved right to do so. I hope this book inspires you to do the same.

This book is like a party where I've invited some of my favourite people, and this introduction is me at the door welcoming you in. We've been talking too long now, though, and you're probably getting cold – so come in! There are some people I'd like you to meet.

1
GRETA THUNBERG

Autistic Climate Activist

Uncompromising is an interesting word. We hear it used all the time to describe great artists, activists and political leaders. But when people talk about autism, they use the phrase 'inflexible thinking', even though uncompromising means the exact same thing. There are loads of parenting websites offering tips on how to help your autistic child to think more flexibly, but a Google search for 'Are autistic people uncompromising?' brings back almost no relevant results.

The rigid and uncompromising thinking we autistic people sometimes have can be good or bad depending on the situation. When I have plans that then need to change, I can find it stressful and I wish that I could be less rigid in my thinking, but when it comes to important political and social causes, we might need people to be less compromising. Neurodivergent climate activist Greta Thunberg thinks it is the flexible thinking of neurotypical people that is destroying the planet. Addressing one crowd of protesters in 2018 she said: 'I have Asperger's syndrome, and to me, almost everything is black and white. I think, in many ways, we autistic people are the normal ones and the rest of the people are pretty strange.'

Greta was born in Sweden in 2003. By her early teens she was already working with a group of activists, planning ways to raise awareness of climate change and put pressure on world leaders to act. The group wanted to organize a protest march, but Greta wanted to put on a school strike (there had been a similar protest in America where children marched out of school to protest gun violence). Greta broke away from the group of activists who she was working with to organize a school strike on her own. She says that if she were not autistic, she might have kept working with the other activists. It's lucky that she didn't because her small protest started a global movement. Soon a photograph of Greta on strike went viral and children all over the world took part in their own school strikes for climate action.

With the movement growing, Greta began meeting with world leaders to discuss global warming. She remained inflexible in her thinking and she always spoke her uncompromising opinions without worrying about whom they might upset. At the UN climate change conference, she told politicians that they were scared of being unpopular but that she was not. She also said that the politicians were stealing from their children's future, which is a pretty confrontational thing to say. I imagine a lot of people wouldn't say things like this to powerful people, because they would worry about being disrespectful.

Greta doesn't worry about being disrespectful. She thinks that it's important not to worry about what we can and cannot say, but to speak clearly. In 2019 she told another group of politicians that they were acting like 'spoiled irresponsible children' for expecting the next generation to deal with climate change. She can speak the truth in this uncompromising way because of her neurodivergent brain. When she was asked by TV reporters what gave her the confidence to speak truth to power, she said, 'I am on the autism spectrum so I don't really care about social codes in that way.'

Later in 2019, Greta travelled to America to speak about the importance of fighting climate change. Legions of angry Twitter users unable to do the most basic research came out to criticize her. Tweeting stuff like 'WELL IF SHE CARES SO MUCH ABOUT CLIMATE CHANGE THEN WHY DID SHE GET A PLANE TO AMERICA? #HYPOCRITE.' Well, actually, she didn't. Greta spent two weeks (each way) sailing on a zero-carbon emissions boat showing her commitment to the cause. While many activists (myself included) are flexible with doing the right thing because being ethical is nowhere near as convenient as Amazon Prime, Greta's rigid and uncompromising thinking has meant that she's one of very few activists who not only talks the talk but walks the walk (or sails the sail?), without ever taking a day off.

Greta continues to speak to world leaders and organize political action, including more school strikes. Now, millions of school children are taking part in 185 different countries. This is only the beginning of the story of Greta Thunberg. It's been only a few years since her original school protest, but in that time she has been twice nominated for the Nobel Peace Prize and listed as one of the most powerful women in the world.

I have an autistic friend who, after seeing what Greta has achieved, posted on Instagram saying, 'I wonder what I might have done if I hadn't spent so much energy learning how to smile when I talked.' Older (but not that much older) neurodivergent people are watching Greta do incredible things with her autistic traits, rigid thinking and disregard for social codes. Many are being inspired to stop wasting their energy trying to change the way they are and start thinking about how to use the way they are to achieve great things.

Greta is one of the youngest people in this book (18 years old at the time of writing); she was born five years after the term 'neurodiversity' was coined. She's part of a new generation of neurodivergent people who aren't waiting until they're adults to see their differently wired brains as something to be proud of. What's even more exciting is that she has a huge social media reach, which she uses to spread the word directly. She uses her social media platforms to raise awareness of climate change and speak about the benefits of neurodivergent thinking.

This generation of neurodivergent people will be unlike any generation that came before it. They will be the first to grow up hearing that being different is a superpower, and with an impending climate emergency, they have arrived just in time.

Discussion questions for your school, college or book club

→ Which people (either famous or whom you know personally) would you describe as uncompromising?

→ What situations might it be good for someone to think about in an uncompromising, 'black and white' way?

→ What are the benefits of being direct and not worrying about hurting people's feelings?

2
MICHAEL BUCKHOLTZ

Autistic Music Producer and Campaigner

Michael Buckholtz has a CV that is longer and more varied than the CV of anyone else I know. I've just got one chapter to tell you about his time in the military, his time writing and producing music for a rap megastar, his activism and his plans to build a ground-breaking music studio. The common theme is that his approach to all of these has been driven by his autistic traits. Some might not think of self-belief and lack of fear as obvious autistic traits because they don't fit the stereotype of autism, but Michael has never fitted stereotypes.

Michael was born in 1965 to a military family. Things were very regimented; he had to fold his bedsheets with what were called 'hospital corners'. His father also insisted that Michael was polite, which meant lots of eye contact and shaking hands, two things Michael found difficult. His passion for music was there from a young age. He learned to play clarinet, then other instruments, and by the time he was 14 he was playing bass guitar in the family band. His brother would play electric guitar, some neighbourhood friends would play drums and keyboards, his younger sister and brother rapped, and the whole thing was organized by his mother as a way for the family to connect.

School was tough for Michael. He found lessons boring, and as he got older, he started getting bullied. He felt like an outcast and decided to take extra classes so he could leave school as quickly as possible. At 16 he found himself interning at the local TV station, then shortly after that he joined the US Navy.

At 18 he was stationed in Japan where he met another young man called Kirk, better known now as hip-hop superstar MC Hammer. Kirk was like an older brother to Michael; he saw that Michael was different, looked after him and even loaned him money to buy instruments. Michael's relationship with the military was coming to an end, but his relationship with Kirk lasts to this day.

Michael left the military and got his first proper civilian job as a radio DJ. Shortly after that, Michael reconnected with Kirk, who was also working in the music industry. He decided to pack up his belongings (including all his musical instruments) and head across the country to California where he was signed by Kirk's new record label, Bust It Records. Soon Michael was writing and producing for MC Hammer as well as other musicians on the label.

When Michael first moved to California, he was living in his car, but now he was working on some of the most popular music of the time. One of the records he worked on, 'Please Hammer Don't Hurt 'Em', went diamond, selling more than ten million copies (the first rap record to do this). Since then, the album has sold over 50 million copies (roughly the equivalent of every person in Australia owning two copies each).

In 1999 Michael received a letter from some friends. They'd been reading about autism and recognized a lot of what they'd read in Michael. Michael sent the same information to his mum back home. It explained so much about what she had experienced with Michael and his siblings that she cried as she read it. This prompted Michael to seek an official diagnosis, which answered so many questions for him. It helped him to accept himself and know that he wasn't 'losing his mind'.

Michael had always known about the mistreatment of black people in America. He'd experienced it first-hand, especially from the police. His hyper-focused empathy meant that he cared about all racial injustice he saw, heard or read about. He knew that being black in America is hard enough, but being black and autistic adds another layer of barriers for people.

Michael had to speak out about how black autistic people were treated. There wasn't a lot of mainstream representation of autistic people, and what there was tended to show only white boys. This meant that if you were autistic but weren't white, then you weren't getting noticed. To redress this, Michael wrote a book called *Autism Is My Universe*, detailing his experiences of being autistic and black in America.

Just as he had thrown himself head first into the military and then the music industry, Michael jumped into a new chapter in his life as an activist and advocate for autistic people. He started the Aid for Autistic Children Foundation (AACF), a charity which helped autistic people and their families cope with the financial burden of living in an ableist society. He even went on hunger strike to raise awareness of this cause. Michael then got involved with the disability rights organization Yes I Can (YIC) Unity, who push to get young disabled people jobs in the entertainment industry. Michael puts himself out there to inspire young autistic people and to speak out about racist and ableist injustice.

My favourite thing about Michael is that he doesn't just talk about autistic people being included; he goes out and does something. At the time of writing, he has just found a location for his new music studio, designed especially to be accessible to autistic people. I can't wait to see what Michael does next. Whatever it is, we know that he will run at it head first and that he will be guided by autistic hyper-focused empathy.

Discussion questions for your school, college or book club

→ What do you think are the stereotypes of autistic people?

→ In what way does Michael break those stereotypes?

→ Where do you think those stereotypes come from?

→ In what ways are those stereotypes harmful?

3
WARREN FRIED

Dyspraxic Founder of Dyspraxia USA

It's Labor Day weekend in September 2006 and Warren Fried is about to host his first ever gathering of dyspraxic people. The venue is booked. The invites have gone out. The press are in. Everything is in place for one of the first opportunities ever for dyspraxic Americans to come together and share their experiences of an often-misunderstood condition.

Unfortunately, no one showed up.

Warren wasn't put off, though. He confidently told the local paper about his plans to put on more events.

Born in New York, Warren spent his teenage years in Florida. From a young age he knew he was different to the other kids, but he couldn't work out what made him different (and nor could anyone else). He didn't seem to fit into any of the disability boxes, and he looked and sounded just like everyone else, but there were some things he found really difficult. He struggled memorizing things and judging distances; it was as if he could only see in 2D. This meant safely crossing roads was a challenge, as was walking down the street without bumping into people. Even when playing board games, Warren found he couldn't place the pieces where they were supposed to go. Like many neurodivergent children, Warren was bullied for being different and, growing up, he struggled with his mental health.

At 18, Warren moved to the UK to attend university. While he was there, the staff looked at his notes from back home and told him that he was dyspraxic. That word changed everything. Finally, he knew why he was different, and everyone else could understand why too. This would be the beginning of a new era in Warren's life

Warren spent the next five years travelling around the UK, meeting dyspraxic people and learning everything he could. The first other dyspraxic person he met was Mary Colley, who had written one of the most famous books about dyspraxia. Warren learned so much from Mary that he would go on to name an award after her. There were groups already set up for dyspraxic people in the UK, so it was easy to get stuck in with meeting people through charities and support groups.

Armed with this new sense of understanding, he returned to America where he discovered that dyspraxia was not as well known as it was in the UK. In fact, when Warren attended a disability pride parade, they thought that he was making the condition up!

Warren's empathy went into overdrive. He decided to set up an organization that would offer support to dyspraxic people, raise awareness and educate those in positions of power. And so Dyspraxia USA was founded. Warren had only just started the organization when he held the event where no one turned up.

When Warren told the press that more events would happen and people would be helped, he was right. Now, just a few years later, there are meet-and-greet events in Michigan, Kentucky, Illinois, Pennsylvania, Florida, Colorado... I won't list them all – there's a lot! He has proved anyone who doubted him wrong.

Warren now lives in northern Illinois with his wife and their children. He works full time for the organization. He has lectured to the heads of the US Department of Special Education and provided educational sessions for the US Senate. Warren spends the rest of the time supporting dyspraxic people all over America – from families in remote farming communities, to movie stars, to his own twins. Dyspraxia USA is now the go-to organization for people wanting to better understand and support dyspraxic people.

Imagine if Warren had given up in 2006, when no one showed up for his meet-and-greet event – there are so many people who would be worse off if he had. Of course, there was never any question of Warren giving up because of his most powerful neurodivergent trait – drive. Throughout his life, Warren has found things difficult, but what he's learned is that if you find something difficult and keep trying, you will get there eventually. Whether it's working the tumble dryer, cooking a meal or single-handedly running a national charity. That's why he told the press that more events would happen, because just like everything Warren finds difficult, he knew that if he kept on trying, he would get it right eventually.

Some driven people are driven by fame or money, but Warren is driven by another of his powerful neurodivergent traits – empathy. Empathy is the fuel that gives Warren his superhuman drive. He wakes up in the morning feeling what other people are going through and is unable to sit back and watch as dyspraxic people struggle with a lack of support and understanding.

Warren always thinks BIG! His most recent project is a feature-length movie, and he's even talked about starting a university specifically for dyspraxic people. With neurodivergent empathy and drive, it seems like he can do anything!

Discussion questions for your school, college or book club

→ What was it about Warren that meant he didn't give up when no one came to his event?

→ Do you know someone who you would describe as 'driven'? What are they driven by?

→ What difference does awareness of a neurodivergent condition make?

4
FAHIMA ABDULRAHMAN

Dyslexic Video Journalist

I hear people say 'be yourself' all the time. It's the advice we give people when they're going on a date or to a job interview. I was even given this advice by a previous agent when I went for an acting job, which I felt showed a very poor understanding of what acting is all about (I didn't get the part). I guess people need reminding a lot because there can often be a lot of pressure in the world to do the opposite: change yourself to fit in. That's why I wanted to tell you about Fahima Abdulrahman, someone who has stayed true to herself against immense pressure to change.

Fahima was born in Somalia, but because of the civil war she and her family fled when Fahima was a child. Fahima spent most of her childhood in Syria. It was here that she first realized that she was differently wired. In lessons the children would read Arabic poems aloud. Fahima LOVED this and her hand would always be the first to go up to volunteer. When she read aloud, the words would get mixed up. Her teacher assumed that she just wasn't able to read and soon stopped picking Fahima to read aloud.

When she was 16, Fahima moved to the UK. In the UK, when you are 14, you begin studies to take your GCSE exams at 16. If you do well in them and pass the maths and English exams, then you can study for A-level exams at school or college, and if you do well in those, then you can go to university. Those four years can be pretty stressful for young people in the UK. You have to work really hard if you want to go to university. Fahima had to catch up quickly: she had to pass her GCSE English exam in a language she was only just learning to speak. The thought of taking an exam, in a language I'm just learning to speak, designed for people who grew up speaking that language, sounds like something I would have a nightmare about, but in less than two years Fahima had passed GCSE English. A year later she was at university.

Since she was 15, Fahima had known that she wanted to work in the media, so a degree in filmmaking and TV production made sense. It was in the first year of her degree that the university put on a disability awareness week. Fahima discovered that some other students on her course were dyslexic and she started to research what dyslexia is. Bit by bit the pieces started to fit together. Fahima read that dyslexic people often struggle with directions – something that she had always found difficult, too. She also found out that dyslexic people might miss words when they read aloud, just as she did when she was at school in Syria. The more she read and the more she talked to dyslexic students on her course, the more things started to add up.

Fahima likes telling true stories. She comes from a culture where storytelling is an important way to preserve history. Knowing that she found writing difficult but had a passion for telling important stories, she decided to pursue a career in video journalism, working for the BBC.

One of Fahima's first projects was a podcast telling the story of Dina Ali Lasloom. Dina Ali is a Saudi woman who tried to run away from the sexist 'guardianship' rules in her home country. These rules say that a woman can't do all sorts of things including travelling or getting married without the permission of her male family members. In April 2017 Dina Ali was stopped on her way to Australia where she planned to claim asylum. Her uncles took her back to Saudi Arabia and she hasn't been seen since.

Fahima went on to share more stories about how women were being treated in Saudi Arabia; so did lots of other journalists, and social media helped to spread the word with the #SaveDinaAli hashtag. Guardianship laws are still in place, although the Saudi

Royal Family has been forced to roll them back a little bit. Because the stories of people like Dina Ali are being heard, pressure is growing to get rid of these rules completely.

There are loads more incredible true stories that Fahima has shared through her video journalism. I'd love to tell you about them all but I don't have space – for example, there's the Syrian refugee who lived in an airport for months, the first UK mayor to wear a hijab and the jazz singer being threatened with deportation even though she was born in Glasgow.

Fahima knows the importance of telling a story properly and that includes her own. As a black Muslim neurodivergent woman from a refugee background, she has faced huge amounts of prejudice in her career. There was a lot of pressure when writing emails or scripts for Fahima to use correct grammar and spelling to sound professional – if she didn't, then it was easy for some people to dismiss her as uneducated, especially because of her background. She has met many snobby and prejudiced people who didn't take her seriously because of how she wrote or because she listened to audiobooks instead of reading. But once a few good producers recognized how good her work was, Fahima realized that she had proven to herself that she was good, and she didn't need to prove it to ignorant people.

It's a common theme among successful neurodivergent people: we've (I was going to say 'they've' here, but I'm successful too!) made the decision to ignore the pressure to be like everyone else. We know that if we pretend to be neurotypical, then we aren't being true to ourselves, but standing out and being different is great. Fahima has stood out most of her life, because of her race, religion and where she is from, so she's quite happy to stand out for being neurodivergent, too.

If you try to be someone you're not, then you're always going to fail, so just be yourself (unless you're going for an acting job).

Discussion questions for your school, college or book club

→ Would Fahima's life have been easier if she had tried harder to fit in?

→ Can you think of a time when you have been pressured to change who you are to fit in?

→ What things can make it easier for neurodivergent people to be themselves?

5
PIP JAMIESON

Dyslexic Entrepreneur

Neurodivergent people can have a complicated relationship with work. Like many of us, I have had the experience of losing a job because of my neurodivergent traits. Most neurodivergent workers say that they have faced discrimination in the workplace. One report found that 50% of managers would be uncomfortable hiring us in the first place. I don't believe that neurodivergent people are bad workers – we have unique skills and can be incredibly passionate. I believe that the barriers come from the way that employers and workplaces don't include us. Maybe that's why so many of us thrive when we work without a boss. Pip Jamieson has built a successful business without a boss and without compromising on doing the right thing.

Pip was born in New Zealand to British parents. Her father worked in the music industry and she spent her childhood travelling the world with him. When she was a child, her teachers thought she was stupid – they even said so in front of her and her parents. But Pip's mum wasn't having any of it; she knew that Pip was clever. She researched dyslexia and at eight years old Pip was diagnosed. The secondary school Pip went to had a special unit for dyslexic pupils. The school told her about some inspiring dyslexic people, which changed the way she saw the condition.

Pip's parents wanted her to grow up to work in the creative industries, but she rebelled and studied economics at university. After leaving with a first-class degree, Pip worked in lots of exciting jobs, including for the former Home Secretary David Blunkett and in marketing for MTV in Australia. She once helped put on a hip-hop show on an aeroplane!

When Pip worked at MTV, she found it really hard to hire people with the right skills. She could find people through word of mouth, but this meant that the people who were being hired all came from the same backgrounds. So, in 2009, she quit her job at MTV to start The Loop, a networking website for people in creative industries. The business was a success and more than 130,000 creative people use it to find work.

A few years later she moved to the UK to set up The Dots from her new home – a houseboat in London. The Dots is a similar networking website for creative people. When raising money for the business, Pip would often face sexism from potential investors. When she went to meetings with a male colleague, people would assume that he was the CEO, not her. Despite this adversity, her new company raised £4 million from investors by the end of 2017 and continued to grow.

Pip had seen how the people who were hired by MTV all came from similar backgrounds, so she made sure that when employers looked for people to employ on The Dots, they could find talented people from a diverse range of ethnicities, both men and women. She also made sure that LGBT+ people were included.

The Dots has grown and now has half a million people signed up to the website. Ten thousand businesses use it to find workers and the company is worth £13 million. Pip has shown that the creativity and outside-the-box thinking associated with dyslexic people can give you the edge in the world of business.

Discussion questions for your school, college or book club

→ What are the barriers that neurodivergent people face in the workplace?

→ What can employers do to remove those barriers?

→ What are the potential benefits of employing a neurodivergent person?

6
JESSICA THOM

Writer and Performer with Tourette's Syndrome

When I worked with young people, teaching them about neurodiversity, they would often ask me about specific conditions and diagnoses, saying, 'Does this count as neurodiversity?' I understood the question and the reasons for asking. For those young people, the diagnoses they'd been given granted them access to some services and support but denied them access to others. I imagine their diagnoses must have felt like backstage passes at a festival – 'Sorry, your pass just says dyslexia; that gets you into the backstage area but not into the VIP area – you'll need autism or higher to get in there.'

What I love about neurodiversity is that it's not something you need to qualify for. There's no one at the door with a list of conditions that are and aren't allowed in. Tourette's syndrome often gets missed off lists of neurodivergent conditions, but Jessica Thom celebrates it as an important part of neurodiversity. Neurodiversity is an idea and a way of looking at the world that anyone can pick up and use. Jessica calls the big ideas that have shaped her life 'emotional grab rails'. Finding them has helped her to become a critically acclaimed performer, writer and real-life superhero (although the true identity of Touretteshero has never been 100% confirmed).

Even as a child, Jessica knew that her brain worked in a different way. She had been identified as dyslexic and dyspraxic. She also had vocal and physical tics (meaning she made involuntary movements and sounds). Jessica found ways to mask, such as sitting on her legs for so long that she gave herself pins and needles and wouldn't feel like she needed to move. During library sessions at school, she would secretly look for a book which might explain why her brain was different – she never found one.

When Jessica was due to take her GCSE exams at 16, she realized that the way she was being taught didn't work for her. She started making colourful posters with the facts she needed to learn on them. She put them up around the house and would read them whenever she walked past. This new way of learning meant that Jessica did much better than anyone expected and stayed on at school when this hadn't been the plan. This experience made her realize that adults didn't always know best about what she needed. She started to record lessons and listen back to them while walking her dog. She couldn't concentrate in the classroom, but moving around meant that she could access those lessons in a completely different way.

In her 20s, Jessica's tics intensified, having a bigger impact on her life. She was diagnosed with Tourette's syndrome (sometimes shortened to Tourette's). There's a stereotype that Tourette's means people swearing involuntarily. The term for the involuntary use of obscene or unacceptable language is coprolalia. In fact, only 10% of people with Tourette's have coprolalia. Jessica is one of them, although most of her vocal tics are more U-rated. 'Biscuits' is a common tic, which she can say 16,000 times a day.

Jessica had to learn to advocate for herself. Finding the right language was important in helping her do this. So was an idea (or emotional grab rail) called the Social Model of Disability. The Social Model of Disability says that what makes disabled people's lives tough is not their conditions or differences but the social barriers and prejudices in the world. Jessica saw how this applied to her own life.

Another big idea came from her friend Matthew, who described her tics as a 'crazy language generating machine'. He said that it would be a waste for Jessica not to do something creative with her tics. 'Crazy language generating machine' is a great description of Jessica's vocal tics, many of which are poetic, beautiful and funny. My personal favourites are 'Do you want to imagine a bear having sex with a keyboard?' and 'Bryan Adams is allergic to his own sheep'.

Jessica and Matthew started Touretteshero, an organization set up to celebrate and share the creativity and humour of Tourette's. They set up a website where they could share some of Jessica's tics so that other people could enjoy and be inspired by them. Jessica wrote a regular blog where she talked about what it was like having Tourette's. She talked about her negative experiences of social barriers, ignorance and discrimination, but also the wonderful experiences she had with friends and her spontaneous interactions with strangers. Jessica and Matthew put on events for children and young people with Tourette's, often attended by Touretteshero herself, a mysterious figure in a blue mask and cape who looks (and tics) a lot like Jessica.

As the blog started to gain popularity, it caught the attention of comedian and writer Stephen Fry, who invited Jessica to be on a TV show he was making about language called *Planet Word*. Soon a publisher wanted to make a book from Jessica's blogs. The book would be called *Welcome to Biscuit Land* in a reference to Jessica's most recurring tic.

Jessica's creativity combined with her 'crazy language generating machine' continued to create amazing work. Her next project would be a live show called *Backstage in Biscuit Land*, which used puppetry, stand-up and storytelling inspired by tics. Jessica made sure that every performance was 'relaxed', meaning that people who faced barriers going to other theatre shows could attend this one.

Jessica now makes regular TV, radio and podcast appearances, where she talks about her experiences and why neurodiversity is important (her appearance on one TV show has over a million views online). She's currently planning a sequel to *Backstage in Biscuit Land*.

Big ideas like neurodiversity and the Social Model of Disability have shaped Jessica's life and work. The exciting part is that no one owns those ideas – they are free for anyone to use as emotional grab rails.

Activity for your school, college or book club

Here are some of my favourite tics from the Touretteshero website. Use them to inspire your own creative projects – artwork, comedy sketches, poetry or something else.

→ 'Lamp post, are you playing hide and seek?'

→ 'Rubber ducks at dawn.'

→ 'Steal a dog, take it to the circus, train it to do Mum's Christmas shopping.'

7
FARAH NANJI
(AKA DJ NINJA)

Dyspraxic DJ and Racing Driver

Here's what you need to understand about house DJ and racing driver Farah Nanji. She has a spiky profile of skills, which means that there are some things she's really good at and some things she struggles with a lot. She struggles with coordination, which is essential for both DJing and racing. But for Farah, passion and drive meant she could overcome any barrier. In fact, her spiky profile of skills means that she approaches her passions in new and innovative ways.

At school there were some lessons in which Farah excelled, like English, religious studies and history. But in other subjects, like maths and design, things just didn't seem to work. The teachers saw this and assumed that, in the lessons where she struggled, either she wasn't trying or she was deliberately misbehaving. It wasn't until she was 15 that she was diagnosed with dyspraxia, and even then she didn't receive much support.

Farah had to make her own way through a very pressurized school system. This meant doing what she calls 'rewiring'. In a lesson she found difficult – maths, for example – she would break a problem down into smaller parts. When looking at an equation, she would think deeply about what each number and symbol meant. Then she would work up from there to do the larger equation. At school, this rewiring was enough to get her through her exams, but as she grew up, it meant that her brain was built to think differently and come up with new ideas or ways of doing things that no one else had thought of.

Farah's first passion, DJing, started on a car journey with her dad when she was 13. A song came on the radio called 'Push the Feeling On' by Nightcrawlers. It sounded completely different to anything she'd heard before; it was uplifting and happy but repetitive at the same time. From then on she was hooked on house music and at 15 she snuck into a nightclub to hear a live DJ.

Soon Farah had signed herself up to DJ school. It was tough; it took Farah longer to grasp than the other students, which meant that she got left behind. Shortly after finishing DJ school, Farah was offered a summer residency at a club in Mykonos owned by her friend's brother. Farah knew this was an incredible opportunity, but she also knew that she just wasn't ready yet. She turned down the opportunity so that she could spend the summer having one-to-one lessons, polishing her DJ skills in a way that worked for her.

Farah started DJing in prestigious London venues, all while studying at university. Next, she was given an internship by a magazine to go to Ibiza and spend the summer writing about the music and clubbing scene. Her first interview was with Pete Tong, one of the most famous DJs in the world. On returning from Ibiza, Farah began getting more and more high-profile DJing gigs. She went on to perform at some of the most famous clubs in the world and for big organizations like the United Nations Refugee Agency. She produces her own music, too; as I write this, she is working on her debut album.

You might think that Farah has achieved success as a DJ by overcoming her dyspraxic traits, but that's not entirely true. There are parts of DJing that she finds more difficult than others. But her 'rewired' approach means that she is always breaking down problems and finding interesting new ways of doing things. Her fascination with the numbers she would find when breaking down maths problems at school has inspired her debut album. The same neurodivergent traits that meant she struggled at DJ school are now what set her apart from the crowd.

Wired Differently

Remember when I said that Farah was a DJ *and* a racing driver? Well, here's the other half of her story.

Growing up, Farah would spend every Sunday with her grandfather watching Formula One racing. In the week, she would play racing video games after school, and when she was 13 she finally got to drive an actual go-kart. Driving became an escape from school, where she was struggling with many of the lessons and being bullied because she was different.

The dyspraxia diagnosis hit Farah's driving ambitions hard. She knew only a few people can make money from Formula One; fewer than 800 people have ever even taken part in an F1 race. The difficulties associated with dyspraxia and the cost of training to be a Formula One driver meant that she knew this dream was unrealistic. Farah was devastated but she tried to forget about that dream, focusing on music and exams.

When Farah left college at 18, she saw a competition on Facebook to win an internship with the world-famous Gumball 3000 rally. She entered, won and was sent off to help out on the international event. Farah saw a different side of motor racing and realized that there were different ways to pursue a career in racing other than being a driver.

At university, Farah met other students who loved racing as much as she did. She decided to form a racing society so they could all meet and, with her connections from her internship, she could put on events for them. The society evolved into Regents Racing, which still operates today as a private members' club for motorsports fans worldwide.

Farah's ability to break down a problem and build it back up into a solution has meant that she can overcome any adversity. During the 2020 coronavirus lockdown, when nightclubs were closed, Farah made national news as she took to the internet to livestream her DJ sets. Her innovative approach to her motorsports career has also seen her dubbed an 'autopreneur' by Channel 4. The rewiring she did at school has given her the ability to think outside the box and achieve all the success she has today.

Discussion questions for your school, college or book club

→ What do you think is your greatest strength and greatest weakness?

→ Can you think of a time when you have struggled with a task but then approached it in a different way to succeed?

→ Which other successful people can you think of who approached a problem in a way no one had thought of before?

8
NAOKI HIGASHIDA

Autistic Writer

Autistic people often get placed into one of two categories – 'high-functioning' or 'low-functioning'. If you think about it, these categories don't really make a lot of sense. I function pretty well when speaking to a big group of people on a topic I know about. Put me in a small conversation where I have to improvise what to say and make sure I talk a bit but not too much, and I function less well. If I have to do that when I'm tired and in a noisy room while wearing uncomfortable clothes, then I hardly function at all. This is why I always try to leave weddings as early as possible.

Functioning labels aren't helpful. Not because all autistic people are the same (far from it), but because they don't take into account the environment someone is in or the support that they are (or are not) getting. People who are labelled as high-functioning are assumed not to need any support: basically neurotypical but a bit socially awkward. People who are labelled as low-functioning are assumed not to have any capacity to make decisions for themselves or to achieve. Naoki Higashida is someone who might be labelled as 'low-functioning' or 'severe', mainly because he is non-speaking, but his bestselling book *The Reason I Jump* is one of the most popular and critically acclaimed books about autism ever written.

Naoki was diagnosed with autism at the age of five and sent to a school for children with learning difficulties in Kimitsu City (not far from Tokyo in Japan). The teachers there made an 'alphabet grid' for him using cardboard so that he could point at letters. Soon he was writing poems and stories.

When Naoki was 13, he wrote *The Reason I Jump*. In the book Naoki answers questions about what it's like being autistic such as 'Do you prefer to be on your own?' and 'Why can't you have a proper conversation?' In between, he includes some of his short stories.

By the time he was 16, he had written more than ten books but still wasn't allowed to attend his local high school. He appeared in the ground-breaking movie *Wretches and Jabberers* in which two autistic men who communicate using similar techniques to Naoki meet with him and discuss justice and advocacy for autistic people.

It was around this time that Keiko Yoshida found a copy of *The Reason I Jump* and began reading it. She would read out the good bits to her husband, who happened to be the British author David Mitchell. Eventually, they realized that the whole book was good bits. There wasn't an English translation, so they made one themselves which they could share with their own autistic son's carers and teachers. David's publishers found out and in 2013 the English translation became a bestseller.

Keiko and David translated a follow-up book called *Fall Down 7 Times, Get Up 8*, which Naoki wrote when he was in his late teens and early 20s. It features some of Naoki's poems and more short pieces of writing about what it's like being autistic.

The Reason I Jump inspired a film featuring lots of other non-speaking autistic people. More books are being published by non-speaking autistic writers (another of my favourites is *Plankton Dreams* by Tito Rajarshi Mukhopadhyay, where he talks about his experiences in special needs education). Naoki has changed the way that neurotypical people think about non-speaking autistic people and challenged prejudices. Non-speaking autistics are starting to be heard and they have important things to say.

Discussion questions for your school, college or book club

→ What assumptions do you think people made about Naoki because he didn't talk?

→ Some people say that neurodiversity doesn't work for people who might be labelled as 'low-functioning' or having 'severe autism'. Do you think this is true?

→ What needs to change socially so that people like Naoki who aren't famous writers are properly included and valued?

9
BENJAMIN ZEPHANIAH

Dyslexic Poet

Wired Differently

This might be stating the obvious (considering my job) but I *really* love words. I'm not particular about where the words come from. Obviously, books are great, but I love TV with good dialogue, songs with great lyrics and juicy gossip from my friends too. In fact, sometimes the spoken word can be more exciting than the written word; you get an extra something from the way the speaker raises their voice for dramatic effect or pauses before the punchline of a joke. I can pinpoint exactly where my love of the spoken word started. It was when I was 15, on a school trip to a poetry reading, when I saw the dyslexic performance poet Benjamin Zephaniah.

Benjamin was born in 1958. The British school system of the time had little understanding of dyslexia and was very racist. Here's an example: one day at school Benjamin was struggling with some reading. The teacher came over to him. He assumed that she was going to help him, but instead she said, 'Well, you know, not everyone can be really clever; you dark people, you're really good at sport.' She got him a football and told him to go outside to play for the rest of the lesson as the rest of the children watched out of the window.

When Benjamin was given the chance at school, he proved the bigoted teachers wrong. In one lesson the children were asked to each write a story. By the time everyone else had finished, Benjamin had got as far as 'Once upon a time, there was a dog'. At first, he was told off for writing so little. But when the other children stood up to read their stories, Benjamin said, 'I can do that!' He got up in front of the class and made up a story for them. The story was so good that the class could hardly believe that he hadn't rehearsed it. To me, this shows that if neurodivergent people are given a chance to show the things we are good at, then we can blow people away.

Benjamin Zephaniah

The school system carried on missing Benjamin's brilliance, and soon he was getting in trouble with the police. He wasn't perfect, but the justice system was corrupt, and after he left school, Benjamin spent time in prison for a robbery which he didn't do!

It was hard for a young black man to find work in 1970s Britain, where people were more open with their racism, but it was even harder now that Benjamin had a criminal record. Soon he slipped back into crime, managing a group of young men (whom he called his 'boys') who would go out stealing car tools for Benjamin to sell. He wasn't happy. He remembered a teacher who told him that he would either end up dead or in prison, and he was worried that teacher would be proven right. One day, Benjamin made the decision to turn things around; he told his boys he was giving up crime and moved to London to become a poet.

Benjamin's first book of poetry was transcribed by his girlfriend at the time. It was called *Pen Rhythm* and, once he found a publisher, it was an instant hit. A few months later, Benjamin was on TV, where they introduced him as one of Britain's new young black *writers*. The only problem was that Benjamin wasn't able to read or write; he thought that if he was going to be called a writer, he had better learn how to write.

Benjamin enrolled on an adult education course where one of the teachers told Benjamin that he was dyslexic. At first he didn't know what it meant – he thought maybe the teacher was insulting him – but when it was explained to him, he realized why he had struggled at school writing down the story that he could easily stand up and tell the class.

Benjamin doesn't see dyslexia as a disability to be overcome.

In fact, as he started to write more books himself, he realized that being dyslexic made him a better writer, because if he couldn't spell a word, it forced him to think about what other words he could use.

Benjamin continued to perform and write poetry. His performances were very political. At some he would talk about how the police were mistreating black people, and the audience would go straight from the gig to the police station to protest. His popularity grew. He wrote and recorded more poems, then started writing for children and young adults. Benjamin became one of the most famous poets in the country and a role model for dyslexic people. He now spends his time performing, travelling and teaching at Brunel University. He plays Jeremiah Jesus in the TV show *Peaky Blinders* and you'll often see him on political discussion shows speaking truth to power.

Benjamin has a theory that being dyslexic is the default for human beings, and that (even though there are more of them) people who are *not* dyslexic are the unusual ones. He points towards early written languages on cave walls where people would use pictures that looked like the things they were talking about, not symbols to show you what sound to say. The word 'tree' doesn't look like a tree but a cave painting of a tree does. We didn't evolve to tell stories or produce poems by writing them down; we evolved to *speak* them. I think he has a point. In fact, there are many cultures where the spoken word is valued much more than written word, because stories can be passed on from generation to generation.

I realize now that this was what inspired me on that school trip many years ago. The kind of poems that the other poets had written were all contained on the pages and we had to hear them and imagine what they might look like written on a page. They were written in a secret code which only teachers understood, which made them feel like work. Benjamin's poems weren't like that; his poems were meant to be spoken and that made them for everyone!

Discussion questions for your school, college or book club

→ What is your favourite piece of writing that you've only ever heard spoken? (For example, a TV show, joke or a spoken-word poem.)

→ What is it that you like about this writing?

→ Do you think that the writing would be better or worse if it were written down in a book?

10
LYDIA X.Z. BROWN

Autistic Activist and Educator

Wired Differently

Remember at the beginning of this book I wrote about how the word 'neurodiversity' can be used in different ways. Neurodiversity can refer to the fact that people have different brains, but it can also be used to describe a way of looking at the world – one which says that not only is not everyone's brain the same but that there is nothing inherently wrong with any person's kind of brain. Some people try to dismiss this idea as being too radical or extreme – Lydia X.Z. Brown finds this laughable.

Lydia is one of the most important activists in the neurodiversity movement, a movement that wants to change the world to make things better for neurodivergent people. From a very young age, they had an innate sense of what is right and wrong and what is worth fighting for. At school, when Lydia or other students in class were being bullied, Lydia knew that this was wrong and that it was the responsibility of people with power to do something about it.

By the time they went to university, Lydia was already writing about neurodiversity. There were some other students who would talk about neurodiversity, but Lydia did a huge amount of work to make sure that it (alongside other important ideas) was being discussed. Lydia led campaigns and became something of a public face for issues relating to disability and neurodiversity at the university.

In Lydia's first year of university they found out about the mistreatment of a boy called Chris Baker. Chris had been tied up in a bag at school after he didn't do what he was told. Lydia heard about what happened to Chris and started a petition demanding the school take action. The school refused to. Lydia was frustrated and disappointed but not surprised.

When some people might give up as their activism is being dismissed or ignored, Lydia doesn't. Lydia believes that we have a moral obligation to keep speaking out. When Lydia learned from other autistic and disabled activists about how disabled people were being subjected to painful electric shocks at the Judge Rotenberg Educational Center, they joined protests to try to stop this from happening.

Other people began to recognize how important Lydia's activism was. In 2013 Lydia was honoured by the White House as a champion of change for disability rights, and the next year received an award for activism from the Washington Peace Center.

In 2017, Lydia was the lead editor on *All the Weight of Our Dreams*, a book containing writing by autistic people of colour. So much writing about autism focuses on white people and the most publicized books by autistic writers are usually by white autistic writers, so *All the Weight of Our Dreams* is a very important book.

Lydia now spends their time writing and speaking about neurodiversity and disability justice. They are still young but they are already one of the most important people in the neurodiversity movement. The neurodiversity movement is growing, and with the help of people like Lydia, I believe it will be hard to stop.

Discussion questions for your school, college or book club

→ Why do you think that powerful institutions can be resistant to the neurodiversity movement?

→ Lydia believes that whatever resources a person has to challenge injustice, we have an obligation to use those. What resources do you have to challenge injustice?

→ How can you use the resources available to you to challenge injustice?

11

SAMANTHA STEIN
(AKA YO SAMDY SAM)

Autistic YouTuber

Wired Differently

Over the summer of 2020 I binge-watched every video by the autistic YouTuber Yo Samdy Sam. In the videos she talks about everything autism-related: assessments, coping with change, noise sensitivity, and even the history of autism and witchcraft!

My favourite video is the one on 'masking'. 'Masking' is the term used to describe when neurodivergent people do things to appear more neurotypical. In the video, Yo Samdy Sam talks about how masking can have a negative impact on the mental health of autistic people. I can spend a lot of energy masking, and it leaves me feeling completely drained sometimes. If I have a meeting where I force myself to make eye contact, I have to sit in my car afterwards to recharge. Of all her videos, this is the one I have watched the most because it is so relatable. The video (like everything on Yo Samdy Sam's channel) feels so authentic, probably because she is actually an autistic person.

Samantha Stein (Yo Samdy Sam's real name) was born in Buckinghamshire in England. She went to an all-girls school and, up until the age of 12, she didn't seem that different to the other girls in her class. She was able to speak clearly, she found schoolwork easy and she had a best friend so was never on her own. As she got older and moved up to secondary school, Samantha found social interactions a lot more difficult. The other girls seemed to understand how to socialize in a way Samantha didn't. It was like they'd all been given a rule book but she hadn't. Samantha felt like there was something wrong with her so she decided to 'fix' herself by learning how to interact in the way that the other girls in her school did. Of course, she wasn't really 'fixing' herself (there wasn't anything wrong with her to fix); she was masking who she was to appear more neurotypical.

Samantha Stein (aka Yo Samdy Sam)

As a teenager, Samantha became really good at masking. She studied how neurotypical people socialized from TV shows like *Friends* and *Buffy the Vampire Slayer*. People seemed to like her when she masked and she made a lot more friends.

At 19, Samantha went to university to study psychology. At school she studied lots of different subjects, but here she could focus on one topic that she was really interested in, so it felt like much less work than she had at school. However the pressure to socialize was immense and Samantha threw herself into masking so she could be seen as the most sociable person at university. Masking isn't easy for neurodivergent people; it takes lots of energy to pretend to be someone you're not. All of the masking was tiring and left Samantha feeling completely burnt out.

When she graduated, Samantha struggled to find a permanent place of work; instead, she did lots of temporary office and nannying jobs, and studied part time for a Master's degree. In her limited spare time, she helped set up the UK's first atheist summer camp, Camp Quest, where kids could spend the summer having fun and learning about philosophy and science. The camp made national headlines, was extremely popular and still runs today with dozens of kids attending every year.

Not long after Samantha set up Camp Quest, she was diagnosed with coeliac disease, a condition which could only be treated by cutting all gluten out of her diet. Samantha started The Happy Coeliac, a blog with recipes, reviews and advice on eating a gluten-free diet. The blog went on to inspire Samantha to publish books of her own gluten-free recipes.

Samantha's passion for psychology never went away and she would watch videos on the topic all the time. In 2017 she stumbled across a video by a YouTuber called Invisible I, all about autism in women and girls. This was what Samantha calls the 'lightbulb moment' when everything suddenly made sense. She had read about autism at university but never related to it herself – mainly because all the examples of autistic people they gave at university were men. In fact, she'd even been told that being autistic meant having an 'extreme male brain'. Researching online, Samantha found a list of autistic traits and showed it to her husband; it described her so well that he thought that she had completed an online personality test. Samantha sought an autism diagnosis and on 12 February 2019, she posted the first video on her new YouTube channel called 'Diagnosed with autism...(aged 33!)'. She shared that video with her friends online and pretty soon it had more than 100 views, which Samantha thought was incredible – little did she know that within a couple of years that video would have over 100,000 views. Samantha kept posting videos, and more and more people started watching them. She was starting to build a fanbase.

There are loads of great autistic YouTubers, but what I particularly like about Yo Samdy Sam is how honest and open her videos are. Most of the comments underneath could be summarized as 'I love this because I can relate to it!' – and that's what I love about them too. In the past, neurodivergent people's experiences haven't been seen on television or in film, so now that they are finally being heard, people like Samantha are quickly gaining thousands of fans. At the time of writing, Yo Samdy Sam has over 100,000 subscribers, her top video has 1.5 million views and across all her videos she has racked up over five million views.

Growing up, Samantha spent so much time masking her neurodivergent traits and now she has thousands of fans who admire her because she is so open and honest about who she is. Looking at her life, she's always been different – even when she was trying to be 'normal', she was doing incredible things – so who knows what she will achieve in the future now that she's not trying to 'fix' herself.

Discussion questions for your school, college or book club

→ Is it better to learn about autism from an autistic person, and why?

→ What do you think causes neurodivergent people to mask?

→ What do you think are the impacts of masking for neurodivergent people?

12

BEN COYLE-LARNER
(AKA LOYLE CARNER)

Dyslexic Musician with ADHD

I'm a huge hip-hop fan. I even have a little model of the Notorious B.I.G. on my desk where I write to inspire me. I love the American rappers from that era. They were great storytellers and poets, and they told the truth no matter how grisly it was. They were, however, very macho. They wanted you to know that they were tough and not to be messed with. Mainstream hip-hop has since matured and become a more inclusive genre where people are allowed to be vulnerable. Artists like Loyle Carner have helped make that change happen.

I heard my first Loyle Carner song a few years ago. It started with a slow bassline that goes 'bam-bam bam-bam b-b-b-bam bam bam'. Over that you can hear the bass player's fingers running up and down the strings. Loyle comes in with lyrics which are funny and clever, then the beat comes in, bits of guitar and more rapping. The song was called 'No CD' from his debut album *Yesterday's Gone*. It is a perfect song. I don't know how to make music at all, let alone music that sounds original and exciting, but I imagine it helps to think differently to other musicians. That's why it came as no surprise to me to find out that Loyle Carner is dyslexic and has ADHD.

Loyle Carner's real name is Ben Coyle-Larner. He called himself Loyle Carner in a nod to his dyslexia. Ben grew up in Croydon (which is either in south London or south of London depending on whom you ask), with his mother, stepfather and stepbrother. He was energetic and loved making dinner. By the time he was six or seven, he could cook on his own. His mum saw that cooking focused his spare energies and meant that they had a tasty family meal.

Ben was the only person with brown skin in an otherwise all-white house. At secondary school, he felt like an outsider. He'd end up playing football with the black kids, but when they talked about their African heritage, he'd have to ask what things were.

Ben loved rap music but at this point he was more interested in acting. He got into a very prestigious drama school, but shortly afterwards his stepfather died and Ben dropped out to look after his mum and stepbrother. Ben was in a really low place and would have panic attacks. His mum suggested that he started seeing a counsellor. He was resistant at first but when he went to see the counsellor, his life started getting better and better. It would still take Ben a while before he would talk about this publicly.

Ben was still a brilliant cook so he decided to advertise cooking classes for young people with ADHD. He knew from experience that cooking could be therapeutic for people like him. The cooking classes were successful but Ben's music career as Loyle Carner was taking off big time. He was performing at festivals, opening for huge rappers like Nas and MF Doom, and had been nominated for the BBC's Sound of 2016. A year later he released his debut album, *Yesterday's Gone*. He used the album to talk about important things like love, family and friends; he even had his mum appear on the album reading a poem. The album was nominated for a Mercury Music Prize alongside Stormzy and Ed Sheeran. Critics went wild – one even compared him to Kanye West!

Ben's next album was called *Not Waving, But Drowning*, a reference to a poem by Stevie Smith. Some people have said that Ben is as much a poet as he is a rapper (personally, I don't think poetry and rap are that different). He was inspired by fellow dyslexic poet Benjamin Zephaniah and has read all his novels. The second album was another success. People liked how Ben showed that men didn't have to act a certain way, just because they're men. Men could be sensitive and kind, and respect women.

Ben gave an interview where he talked about seeing a counsellor after his stepfather died. He was becoming increasingly vocal about mental health, especially the ways in which society's expectations of men can have a negative impact on their mental health. He had been made an ambassador for the Campaign Against Living Miserably (CALM), who work to prevent male suicide. When *Not Waving, But Drowning* was released, Ben held an art exhibition to raise money for the cause.

Ben is still young and his career is going from strength to strength. He has challenged what it means to be a man, and his neurodivergent energy can be heard in every second of his music. This sets him apart from other rappers and has made him one of the most exciting recording artists working today.

Discussion questions for your school, college or book club

→ In what ways does Ben challenge stereotypes of how men should act?

→ It's well publicized that men don't talk about their mental health as much as women. Why do you think that is?

→ How do you think that the experience of accessing mental health services like counselling might be different for neurodivergent people?

13

JONATHAN DRANE
(AKA JONO DRANE)

Judoka with ADHD

Wired Differently

It's 2018 and a 30-year-old judoka called Jonathan Drane is giving a TED talk to a packed room in Norwich. The theme of his speech is 'trying'. He tells the audience that our current definition of 'success' fails a lot of us and that we should come up with a different one. I agree: we need a definition of success that isn't just about winning gold medals, having number-one albums and being the first person on Mars. We need one that recognizes people like Jonathan.

Jonathan was born in 1987. When he was 13 years old, he got into judo, training at the same club in Norwich where the Olympic judoka (that's the technical term for someone who does judo) Colin Oates trained. Jonathan hated school; people told him he should be in a 'loony bin'. At 15, he was diagnosed with ADHD, but he'd had no additional support for most of his school life, resulting in feelings of self-doubt and anxiety.

Judo helped him get through his teenage years, and in 2007 he was competing in national tournaments. The next few years would see him travelling as far as Singapore to compete.

In 2011 Jonathan went for a routine eye check where he was diagnosed with corneal dystrophy. His eyesight deteriorated but Jonathan kept competing, moving over to VI (visually impaired) judo. In his first VI judo competition he won gold!

In 2014 Jonathan competed in the ISBA World Championships, a worldwide competition for blind or partially sighted athletes, where he won a bronze medal. That year Jonathan also became an ambassador for the ADHD Foundation. The CEO of the foundation said that his support would help them to 'challenge outdated views associated with ADHD'.

A knee injury meant that Jonathan had to have reconstructive surgery, but nothing was going to stop him from achieving his goal of competing at the Paralympic Games. If his injury meant he couldn't do judo standing, he would do it sitting down. In 2016 Jonathan did travel to Brazil to compete in the Paralympic Games, where he placed fifth in his category. Not long after this he retired from the sport, aged 29.

Onstage in Norwich in 2018, Jonathan told the audience that 'an unused life is not one that has been absent of success, but one that has been absent of trying'. Watching him speak made me rethink what success is. Maybe it's less about winning gold medals and more about someone who continues to train, even when an injury means they have to do so sitting down.

Discussion questions for your school, college or book club

→ What do you think is society's definition of success?

→ How can these definitions exclude neurodivergent and disabled people?

→ What do you think a better definition of success would be?

14
DARA McANULTY

Autistic Naturalist and Writer

The different ways in which some neurodivergent people process sensory information (sound, light, tastes, textures, smells and so on) compared with how neurotypical people process that same information is one of the many ways in which neurodivergence is seen as a problem rather than a difference. Like many autistic people, there are certain sensory experiences that I find horrible but which everyone else seems to be fine with. The main three that come to mind are loud men's voices, sun cream and T-shirts which feel worn (the amount of spare clothes I take on holiday has been described by airport security as 'suspicious').

However, there are lots of examples where sensory differences can be a benefit: they can make you see, hear, taste, feel and smell things in a way that other people don't. Dara McAnulty, the young naturalist from Northern Ireland, processes sensory information differently. He uses that difference to open people's eyes to the beauty of the natural world and the urgent need to protect it.

From a young age, Dara was drawn to the sound of nature. Every buzz, hum or squawk made him want to find out more and understand the world around him. Growing up in Belfast, a big city, those sounds were often drowned out by traffic and aeroplanes. In 2013 Dara's neurodiverse family (his siblings and mum are autistic like him, but his dad isn't) decided to move out to the countryside of County Fermanagh.

Dara loved his new home, where he found quiet places, alive with wildlife, and when he was 12, he started writing about them in a blog. The writing was beautiful, and he knew all the correct names for different animal species (I thought all bees were basically the same, but I was VERY wrong). The blog became hugely popular and won awards from nature organizations.

Dara wasn't just writing about nature; he was writing about the importance of looking after the natural world as it comes under threat from humans. With the help of the naturalist, TV presenter and fellow autistic Chris Packham, Dara got involved in a campaign to protect hen harrier birds from being driven to extinction through hunting. He later attended the launch of Northern Ireland Environment Week alongside important politicians.

As the blog's popularity grew, Dara even appeared on television to talk about it. In 2018, when he was still only 14 years old, he started writing his first book – *Diary of a Young Naturalist*. The book follows Dara's life from spring to spring, exploring the natural world around him, campaigning for the environment and moving to the other side of the country.

I read the book over the summer of 2020 when the UK was in lockdown due to coronavirus. Sitting in my garden with no traffic around, I became more aware of the nature that was all around me: the woodlice bravely crossing our patio, the pigeons constantly on the lookout for local cats...and I swear I once saw bats flying out from a tree two gardens down from us, but no one believes me. Dara's writing was inspiring me to appreciate nature more.

I wasn't the only one reading and being inspired by *Diary of a Young Naturalist*. The book was a hit with readers and critics everywhere. The reviews were glowing and said how incredible it was that someone so young could write so beautifully about nature. The book won the Wainwright Prize for Nature Writing, the An Post Irish Book Award for Newcomer of the Year and the Books Are My Bag Readers Award for non-fiction.

What makes Dara such a great nature writer? Dara has been clear that being autistic is at least one of the reasons. When he was interviewed on the Irish TV channel RTÉ, he said, 'When you pay attention to all of the little details like I do, I think you can sort of gain a greater appreciation for the world that we live in.' Not only is he making people rethink our relationship with the natural world, but he is also changing how we see the sensory differences of neurodivergent people.

Discussion questions for your school, college or book club

→ What might be a benefit to experiencing certain sounds, smells, tastes, textures, colours or light differently?

→ What jobs might require someone to experience these senses more intensely than other people?

→ How can we change the way our schools, colleges or workplaces are set up to include people with sensory differences?

15
RYAN HIGA

YouTuber with ADHD

I don't think we appreciate YouTube enough. Before YouTube, people who wanted to make films and TV had a lot less creative freedom. I've often wondered if this creative freedom benefits neurodivergent people. My theory is that not having a team of TV commissioners telling them what to do means that neurodivergent content creators can produce work in a way that works for them. Although this is just a theory, it is supported by Ryan Higa, one of the most successful YouTubers ever. He has ADHD and his work is bursting with neurodivergent energy.

Ryan was born in 1990. If you had met him as a child, you might not have believed he would become a successful YouTube star (and not just because the website was yet to be launched). He wasn't even the most successful member of his family. He practised judo, but his older brother was much better; Ryan once heard someone refer to him as 'the younger Higa, not the good one'. Ryan hated his brother for saddling him with such huge expectations.

Things were to get even worse when Ryan went to middle school. It was decided that he would go to a different school to his friends, and when he arrived, he saw that he was one of very few Asian kids at the school. Already he stood out as different, and after doing well in a placement test, he was put into a class with older kids. He was bullied relentlessly, called names and tripped up in the corridor.

The bullying was taking its toll on Ryan. His mind went to dark thoughts of death. He didn't think there was any other option and would stay up at night thinking of different ways to kill himself. The only respite he had from these thoughts was watching TV shows and movies. He loved comedies, especially ones with Ben Stiller and Jim Carrey, but also action films and anime cartoons.

After a summer with friends, Ryan realized that it was the bullying he wanted to stop. Ryan started thinking about ways that he could make his situation better. He realized that when the bullies tripped him up and called him names, they would do it for a reason – to make all the other kids laugh. If Ryan could be the funny one instead, then he would take all the power away from the bullies.

Back at school, one of the bullies called Ryan ugly. A few people laughed but then Ryan turned around to the bully and pulled the ugliest face he could (learned from watching Jim Carrey films). 'What, me?' said Ryan and the whole corridor burst into laughter. Ryan had a revelation that would change his life – 'going for the funny' works.

One day, Ryan was at a big family party. Being 13, he was pretty bored but then he saw his mum filming the party on a camcorder. He asked her if he could use it. 'You'd better actually film the party,' she replied. Ryan had an idea: what if he filmed the party from the perspective of an ant? He pointed the lens close to a plate and panned over the napkins and dumplings while doing a dramatic voiceover.

Ryan had found a thing he loved. The following summer would be spent gathering up his friends to collaborate and making longer, more intricate and funnier videos.

Moving up to high school, Ryan struggled to fit in again. At break there would be groups who hung out with people just like them: sporty jocks, goths, popular kids and nerds. He was just Ryan, and there didn't seem to be a group for Ryan. That winter he signed up to the wrestling team and finally had a group of friends who were there for him. Plus he'd found a sport he was good at and where he was inspired to push himself harder.

At the end of Ryan's first year at high school, he found a website that would go on to make him famous – YouTube. The films he had been making were on VHS cassettes. To edit them he had to rewind them, and if someone wanted to watch them, he had to take the cassette round to their house. Ryan convinced his parents to buy a new digital camera so he could edit videos on his computer and upload them to this new website.

Ryan made more videos with his friends and started uploading them to YouTube under the name NigaHiga (Niga meaning 'rant' in Japanese). Ryan started uploading videos and soon people who weren't just friends and family started watching. He was even getting recognized on the street!

The numbers kept rising. By this time Ryan had moved away from home to study nuclear medicine in Nevada. The workload was immense – Ryan had to choose between YouTube videos and his degree. He dropped out of college to make videos full-time and the rest is history. At the time of writing, NigaHiga has more than 21 million subscribers and over four billion video views. Ryan has written his autobiography, he makes music, appears in movies and even has his own charitable foundation.

Ryan's mind works differently to other people's. His ADHD means that he is always thinking of new ideas. Even when he's talking to someone, he might notice an interesting word, then go off on a tangent in his mind about what that word means. When he writes scripts, all of the ideas come at once and he has to make sure he keeps up with them. You can see this in his videos: they're fast-paced with lots of action and jokes.

YouTube has given the perfect space for all of Ryan's neurodivergent ideas to become a reality. It has given a platform to lots of neurodivergent people. I think we're just seeing the start of how the internet will empower incredible neurodivergent creatives.

Discussion questions for your school, college or book club

→ In what ways might having a neurodivergent brain help people working in creative fields?

→ What barriers might neurodivergent people face in creative fields?

→ YouTube is open to everyone. How might this benefit neurodivergent creatives?

16
TEMPLE GRANDIN

Autistic Scientist

Wired Differently

My friend once referred to Temple Grandin as an 'autistic elder'. I loved this expression – it made me imagine a council of wise autistics whom we could go to with our problems. Temple is an important person in neurodivergent history; she introduced ideas to the world that even now are pretty radical but at the time were ground-breaking: the idea that thinking differently can be of benefit to society, that we shouldn't underestimate what autistic people are capable of and that the lived experiences of autistic people are important to listen to. Her CV as an advocate for autistic people is impressive enough, but she is also an animal scientist who revolutionized the way that livestock are treated.

Born in 1947, Temple grew up in an era with less understanding of neurodiversity (in fact, the term 'neurodiversity' wouldn't be invented for around half a century). As a young child, Temple was different to other children. She didn't talk, she would flap her hands, and her tantrums were longer, louder and more furious than those of other toddlers. She spent a lot of time locked in her own world, not responding even to her mother's voice.

Her father thought that she belonged in a hospital (and he wasn't alone in his opinion) but her mother didn't want that. Temple was taken to a doctor who suggested a speech therapist to help her communicate. With the speech therapist's help, Temple started learning to speak, first short sounds like 'ba' for 'ball', but by the time she was five she used full sentences.

Temple started attending a small private school. At her school, the teacher would play music and get the children to clap along. Temple's clapping was out of time; the teacher thought she was doing it on purpose and told her off. The other children laughed at her. The noisy bell, meltdowns and confusing questions from teachers all made school tough for Temple.

Despite this adversity, Temple was able to explore her talents, such as art and making things. She came up with original ideas, like dressing as a dog for the school pet show and getting two other children to pretend to be her masters. Her friend Crystal said that she liked playing with Temple because she wasn't boring.

When Temple moved up to junior high school, the classes were much busier. The school was noisy and the other girls behaved in confusing ways. She was bullied and called names, until one day she threw a book at one of the other girls, hitting her in the eye. Temple was expelled.

Temple's mother had already been in contact with another school. It was a small boarding school where Temple would get a lot of individual attention and there were horses and other farm animals. Temple got on better at this new school, but she had intense panic attacks.

On a school trip, Temple went on a fairground ride called a Rotor. You don't see these much any more, but they look a bit like a giant washing machine turned on its side. People get in and are spun around, and the force of the spin means they stick to the wall. The sensation of being in the Rotor helped Temple feel calm. She was fixated on getting a Rotor ride at school; she even glued up signs on the dormitory walls. The school never did instal a Rotor, but while spending the summer at her aunt's ranch in Arizona, Temple discovered another solution.

Wired Differently

The ranch had a squeeze chute which was used to hold cows in place so they could get shots without kicking out. Temple saw how the pressure of the wooden panels in the squeeze chute calmed the cattle. She thought, 'I've gotta try that', and asked her aunt if she could go in the chute to see if it would relax her too – it did!

Temple would use the chute every day, then when she was back at school, she built her own in her dorm. Some of the staff thought this was weird, and the school counsellor asked if Temple thought she was a cow. But one man felt differently – Temple's science teacher, Mr Carlock. He helped her to test the device scientifically, and she found that many other children found it relaxing. The device went on to be called a 'hug machine' and was sold worldwide to help autistic people relax. Mr Carlock was an important mentor to Temple, who became passionate about science and went on to study psychology and then animal science at university.

Temple's research, design work and new ways of thinking would completely change the way that animals kept for food are treated. She designed a new cattle dip that wouldn't scare the cows and a way to slaughter cattle that was more humane. She worked out how to measure if animals were in distress and check that farmers were treating animals properly.

Temple started attending conferences for occupational therapists and talking about being autistic. The organizer of one of those conferences approached her about writing a book. That book was called *Emergence* and it would become an incredibly important book in autism history. It was one of the first books about autism to be written by an autistic person.

The book was hugely popular, especially with parents who wanted to better understand their autistic children. Shortly after it was published, Temple was at an autism meeting. There were lots of tables, each with a different discussion. Temple was meant to have one table with eight people to speak to, but soon the whole room ended up turning around just to listen to her. Temple would go on to write even more books on autism including *Thinking in Pictures* and *The Way I See It*. She is still one of the most popular speakers and writers on the subject.

All of this would be impressive enough, cementing Temple's status as one of the most important people in autism history. Her life would be the subject of documentaries and even an HBO movie, but Temple is equally important in the history of animal rights. Temple has written books and published papers on animal welfare and now works as a professor of science at Colorado State University. Her work has changed animal lives for the better: over half of all cattle in the US and Canada are handled in places that Temple designed to be humane.

Temple has spoken about the importance of mentors. Her science teacher who encouraged her to test her machine at school was an important mentor to Temple. Through her writing, Temple became a mentor to other neurodivergent people. Her life story is a reminder of how much tougher it was for neurodivergent people in the past and how, by making our voices heard, we can help create a more understanding world.

Discussion questions for your school, college or book club

→ Temple's mother was an important advocate for her, making sure that people didn't give up on Temple. How do you think that Temple's life could have been different if she didn't have someone doing this for her?

→ Do you agree with Temple that it is important for autistic people to find mentors?

→ What do you think makes a good mentor?

17

JESSICA McCABE

YouTuber with ADHD

What makes someone an expert on neurodiversity? Do they need a degree? Do they need to have worked professionally as a psychologist? If so, how long do they need to have done that job for?

The truth is that there are different types of expertise. My friend likens it to understanding mountains. A geologist could study how the rocks formed and a meteorologist could tell you what causes the snow at the top, but to really know what it's like to be at the top of a mountain, you have to ask someone who's actually climbed one. We call this type of expertise 'lived experience' or 'lived expertise' because you can't get it from reading a book or studying at a university; you need to have lived it.

In the past, the only experts on neurodiversity (although the term 'neurodiversity' wasn't being used back then) who were heard were academic experts who had read books about neurodivergent people and studied us from the outside. Then, in the late 20th century, people like Temple Grandin and Polly Samuel started to write books using their lived expertise. This movement grew as more and more people wanted to hear from those with lived expertise. Today, neurodivergent experts on YouTube draw virtual crowds of thousands who want to hear their lived experience. The person with the biggest audience is probably Jessica McCabe, host of How to ADHD.

Jessica was a smart child. She could speak in full sentences before she was two and at school she did very well on tests. She struggled with lots of things too – such as paying attention in class, not losing her things and making friends. As she got older and had more responsibilities with homework and getting to class on time, her grades started to suffer. Her mum took her to a doctor; she was assessed and then diagnosed with ADHD. Jessica started taking medication to help her concentrate and it helped a lot. Her grades improved and she went to college, but then she started to struggle again, dropped out and moved back in with her parents. Over the next ten years, Jessica found it hard to hold down a job. She felt like she had failed.

Jessica started researching so she could better understand what ADHD was and what it meant for her. She found books, websites and podcasts that were useful but tended to be made for parents, teachers or academics studying ADHD. Jessica wanted to make something for people with ADHD, so she started How to ADHD.

To begin with, Jessica would do her own research and then produce videos about ADHD. Then Rachelle (a nurse) and Patrick (an academic) got in touch and offered to help her with her research.

Soon Jessica was calling on various experts to get information for her videos and was bringing her own lived experience, too. Like a heist movie where all the different experts come together to rob a bank, her videos contained all types of expertise and the viewer numbers kept growing. At the time of writing Jessica's channel has over a million subscribers and her videos have been watched over 44 million times.

Many of those views (from the comments, I think, most, but there's no way of knowing for sure) are adults who have ADHD. One viewer said that they cried watching Jessica's video on rejection sensitivity; another uses the videos to explain ADHD to their family.

Jessica combining her lived expertise with the professional expertise in her team to make videos is what is known as 'co-production'. Co-production literally means making stuff together. It's been shown that when people with lived experience and people with professional experience work together designing schools, health services and support for neurodivergent people, they make better decisions than if people with professional expertise did the work on their own. All around the world people are waking up to the importance of co-production. In the UK they've even introduced laws to make sure that it happens. If you're a young neurodivergent person, then I'd urge you to look for opportunities to take part in co-production and share your lived expertise. I can't promise that you'll gain a YouTube following like Jessica's, but you will be sharing valuable expertise that no neurotypical person has.

Discussion questions for your school, college or book club

→ In groups, each think of an experience that you have had which no one else in your group has had. It could be a place you've visited, a ride at a theme park or a live show that you have seen.

→ Each spend some time sharing that experience with the rest of the group.

→ When you have an experience explained to you, think about whether this is the same as having the experience for real. What is the difference between having the experience and hearing about it second-hand?

18
HANNAH GADSBY

Autistic Comedian

I'm focusing on the neurodivergent traits of the people in this book. Obviously I am – it's a book about neurodiversity. But I think it's important to remember that neurodivergence isn't the only part of any person's identity. We're all a mishmash of different identities, experiences and communities. Neurodivergent comedian Hannah Gadsby became an icon for women and LGBT+ people with her ground-breaking stand-up show *Nanette*. She challenged what stand-up comedy could be, and it made people confront how women, particularly lesbian and gender-nonconforming women, are treated in society.

Hannah grew up in a small town in Tasmania (an island off the coast of mainland Australia) where, during her teenage years, being gay was still illegal (at least for men – I don't think anyone had thought to make a law about women). The debate about legalization was happening in the mainstream, and the most horrible anti-gay voices were on TV and in the newspapers. They thought that gay people like Hannah were subhuman. The homophobic looks, words and, on one occasion, violence taught Hannah to hate herself. Her escape was the school library where she loved to read books about art.

Hannah's love of art led to her leaving Tasmania to study art history at university in mainland Australia. After graduation she did lots of different jobs – working in bookshops, at a cinema and as a vegetable picker – before an injury left her unable to work and homeless. She'd had a complicated relationship with her family, but when she picked up the phone, they took her in.

That reconnection with her family led to one of the most important moments in Hannah's life. When visiting her sister in Adelaide (South Australia), she entered a stand-up competition and won! As part of the prize, she was sent to Edinburgh for Festival Fringe, where she entered another competition and came second. Soon Hannah was rising up the ranks of the professional comedy circuit and became known for her hilarious self-deprecating humour.

The irony was that offstage Hannah had always had difficulty turning her thinking into talking – she understood things deeply but struggled to communicate them. Comedy was a way she could communicate her ideas, in a social situation with clear rules: one side speaks the things they have rehearsed, the other side listens.

There's this thing people talk about in comedy called 'punching up or down'. The idea is that some comedy allows people who have little or no power to 'punch up' and make fun of people who have a lot of power. Other comedy 'punches down' and people with power make fun of people who have no power. Hannah's comedy was punching itself: she would make fun of herself, the way she looked and the ways in which she was different to other people. This was a problem for Hannah; she didn't want to do comedy that was self-deprecating, and she didn't want to sugarcoat the experiences of violence and prejudice she had been through because of her gender and sexuality. So she wrote *Nanette*.

Nanette opens with self-deprecating humour as she tells a funny story about someone mistaking her for a man, but then the tone changes. Hannah stops telling jokes; instead, she talks honestly about her experiences and how she's used comedy to make herself more acceptable to a homophobic and misogynist world. The show is intense and uncomfortable to watch, but it's meant to be. It changed what people thought a comedy show could be.

The show won the Barry Award (probably the biggest comedy award in Australia), then it won the Edinburgh Comedy Award (probably the biggest comedy award in Britain), reviews were glowing and every theatre in the world wanted to book Hannah to do the show. When Netflix commissioned a recording of the show, it turned Hannah into a celebrity overnight. Now no one had to queue up for tickets; they could watch the show at home.

In *Nanette*, Hannah says that she is giving up comedy, and in a way she did. She gave up making the kind of comedy where she made fun of herself. Instead, she started doing a new kind of comedy, one that made fun of powerful people.

The follow-up to *Nanette* was a show called *Douglas*, and audiences loved that too. It had a lot more jokes than *Nanette*, but the targets of those jokes were powerful men, not Hannah. In the show she talks about her autism diagnosis. Hannah says that the diagnosis felt like she'd been 'given the keys to the city of me'. It's easy for neurodivergent comedians to make self-deprecating jokes about the ways in which they are different, but Hannah doesn't do this. In *Douglas* she talks about neurodiversity and says that she loves the way that she thinks.

It makes sense that Hannah would love the way that she thinks because she thinks differently, in an industry where being different is the most valuable commodity. That was what made *Nanette* so special; it was just different to other comedy shows, and it challenged the audience to rethink what they were laughing at and who was the butt of the joke. It seems appropriate to me that it was an autistic woman who helped everyone else to think differently.

Discussion questions for your school, college or book club

→ What other things might make up the identities of the neurodivergent people in this book?

→ How might other identities overlap with neurodivergence?

→ What additional barriers might be faced by neurodivergent people from marginalized identities?

19
STEPHEN WILTSHIRE

Autistic Artist

There's a BBC documentary called *The Foolish Wise Ones*. It was broadcast in 1987, so some of the language hasn't aged well (nor have some of the haircuts), but it's still worth watching if you can find it. It follows three autistic men (well, two men and one young boy) who each have an incredible skill. The footage is cut up with neurotypical experts telling you how impressive their talents are. The neurotypicals all seem very confused that someone could be so talented at one thing when they struggle with other things.

The highlight of the documentary, for me, is Stephen Wiltshire. Stephen is just 11 at the time but already an incredible artist. He goes to see St Pancras Station, an old Victorian building in the centre of London, which he'd never seen before. Then, back in the classroom, he draws an almost perfect picture of it. The presenters marvel at how perfect Stephen's understanding of perspective is: the buildings he draws look 3D without using any shading. They keep reiterating the point that Stephen has a low IQ, as though that makes his artistic abilities miraculous. I was struck watching it by how neurodivergent people are so often defined by the things that they can't do rather than the things they can. This doesn't happen with neurotypical people. No one says 'Sure, Beyoncé's good at singing but she's rubbish at table tennis!'

Stephen was born in 1974 to West Indian parents. At the age of three, he was diagnosed as autistic and went to a special school where he developed his love for drawing. He drew animals, cars and caricatures of the staff at school (which, luckily, they found funny). Eventually, he found the subject matter he would become most famous for drawing – buildings. A teacher saw how talented Stephen was and entered his drawings into art competitions. Soon Stephen became a local celebrity; some people couldn't believe that the drawings were really done by him.

In 1987 *The Foolish Wise Ones* was broadcast, and Stephen became nationally famous. Hugh Casson, the famous architect and artist, said that Stephen was 'possibly the best child artist in Britain'. A book was published of Stephen's drawings called *Drawings* (I guess you don't need an exciting book title when the art itself is so good). The book was a hit and lots more would follow.

The next year Stephen went to New York with his teacher and a film team. He met Oliver Sacks, a leading expert in autism. Oliver asked Stephen to draw his house, Stephen stepped outside briefly and then drew Oliver's house perfectly. The drawing is placed at the very start of Stephen's second book – *Cities*.

Stephen kept travelling, and his drawing style became more and more sophisticated. He visited cities in Europe like Venice, Amsterdam, Leningrad and Moscow and drew more for his next book, *Floating Cities*, which was published when he was still just 16 years old.

The following years saw Stephen travelling all around the world to Japan, America, Hong Kong, Spain, Israel, Australia, Turkey, Mexico and more. He would sometimes be flown in a helicopter over a city, so he could take it in and then do a detailed and accurate drawing when back on the ground. His first solo exhibition was held in London and 40,000 people came to see it. In 2005 he drew a 10-metre-long drawing of Tokyo from memory, the longest drawing he'd ever done.

The year 2006 was eventful for Stephen: he was awarded an MBE for his services to art AND he opened his own gallery. The gallery is still open (although it's moved location), and people travel from all around to visit.

Stephen's drawings are so detailed that people can pick out exact places they have visited. My favourite drawing shows the River Thames in London, looking down from above the Houses of Parliament. I've visited that part of London lots of times before.

Stephen keeps pushing his art further. A recent film called *Billions of Windows* shows him using new technology to draw in 3D. Watching the film, I noticed how differently people talk about him now compared with when *The Foolish Wise Ones* was made. In 1987 everyone felt the need to talk about the things that Stephen struggled with; now they just talk about the art.

Neurodivergent people still get defined by the things they can't do, instead of the things they can, but Stephen's commitment to his unique artistic skill has meant that people no longer know him just as a boy who wasn't able to speak fully until he was nine. They know him as the man who drew New York from memory and thousands of people came to see.

Discussion questions for your school, college or book club

→ What are the commonly used definitions of neurodivergent conditions such as ADHD, autism, dyslexia, dyspraxia or Tourette's syndrome?

→ Do these definitions include things that people are able to do or things that people struggle with?

→ How could these definitions be rewritten to include potential skills that neurodivergent people might have?

20
POLLY SAMUEL
(AKA DONNA WILLIAMS)

Autistic Writer

I sometimes hear people refer to the 'autistic community', which conjures up an image in my mind of us all living on a farm together and growing organic vegetables. I don't know if we need to go that far but I believe there is real value in neurodivergent people meeting and spending time together. Today, peer support groups and online networks are commonplace and connect neurodivergent people with shared experiences, but this wasn't always the case. Polly Samuel's work had a huge impact on neurodivergent (and neurotypical) people. For me, her most important contribution was as a founding member of what we now recognize as the autistic community.

Here's a thing you need to know before we start this chapter. For most of her life Polly was known by the name Donna Williams. Towards the end of her life she preferred to be called Polly and took her husband's surname, Samuel. So that's what I've called her here. However, if you want to find her work, it can be easier to search for the name Donna Williams.

Polly was born in 1963 in Australia to an alcoholic mother. Polly was autistic, but because of the poor understanding of autism at the time, she was diagnosed as a 'psychotic child' at the age of two. Polly was abused as a child and young adult. She was kicked, punched and had her hair pulled at home. At school she was called 'disturbed', and as she grew up, she was targeted by abusive men.

With all the abuse she had faced, Polly reached a point of absolute despair. She wrote about her experiences to explain what was going on for her, but she didn't have any plan to publish her writing – in fact, she was going to destroy it. Somehow it found its way to Frances Tustin, an expert in autism, who helped publish it under the title *Nobody Nowhere*. The book became a bestseller and was translated into more than 11 different languages. It was one of the first books to be written by an autistic person about their experiences.

Polly would go on to write a follow-up book called *Somebody Somewhere,* then more books, poems and even music. I could list them all but I think the more interesting story is the story of how the books, writing and music were received and the massive impact they had on changing how autistic people see themselves. You see, because Polly was writing from an inside perspective as an autistic person, her work helped other autistic people to recognize experiences they'd had as autistic experiences.

In the early 1990s an 'autistic community' was forming and Polly's work was at the centre of it. A couple of autistic people in America had read Polly's book and worked with her to found the Autism Network International (ANI). Where other support and advocacy groups were run by non-autistic people, the ANI was run by and for autistic people. The way they would talk about being autistic was different to other groups. too. In their newsletter they published an article by Jim Sinclair called 'Don't mourn for us', which said that parents shouldn't be sad when they find out their children are autistic because it is part of who their child is. At the time this was a pretty radical idea – and, for some people, it still is today.

Polly knew that other people like her were out there, and she had to find them. She would make an effort to spend time with other autistic people, sharing experiences and doing things they enjoyed such as looking at sparkly objects. She would hold autistic dinners, inviting autistic people to get together to meet. Polly also helped to invent language to describe parts of the autistic experience. My favourite term is a 'gadoodleborger', which is a person who can be a bridge-keeper between different types of normality. I think maybe Polly was a gadoodleborger because her writing was picked up by neurotypical people and it helped them to understand what it was like being autistic.

In 2016 Polly was diagnosed with terminal breast cancer and a year later she passed away. When people die, we always talk about how they live on through the people whose lives they changed, and it's undeniably true for Polly. Her role in getting autistic people to recognize themselves and each other changed the course of history.

Polly inspired so much of what we now call the autistic community. She did this by telling people that neurodivergent minds are brilliant, not just when they program computers or design buildings (although that's pretty cool, too), but they are brilliant just on their own as unique and beautiful things. The community which she had an integral part in building played a leading role in the neurodiversity movement. I believe that Polly will be remembered as an important historical figure, someone who brought people together so that those people changed the world.

Discussion questions for your school, college or book club

→ Polly called people who could bridge between different types of normality 'gadoodleborgers'. Who do you consider to be a gadoodleborger?

→ Why is it important for neurodivergent people to be able to meet each other and share experiences?

→ Can you think of a time when someone has told you about an experience that you could relate to? How did this feel?

21
ANN BANCROFT

Dyslexic Explorer

There's a famous quote from George Mallory about why he chose to climb Mount Everest. He said 'because it's there'. Which sounds really cool, but if I had been there when he said it, I'd have replied, 'Yes, it is there, but it's also really cold, tall and you might die climbing it.' Explorers see parts of the world that are so difficult to survive in that only a handful of people have been before and they say, 'I wonder what's over there?' Most people don't choose to go exploring in dangerous parts of the world, so those who do must have very unusual brains. It isn't a surprise to me that Ann Bancroft, one of the most important explorers alive today, is also neurodivergent.

Ann began leading expeditions when she was just eight years old, taking her cousins on backyard winter camping trips in Minnesota, where she spent most of her childhood. She loved exploring the natural world.

Ann's neurodivergence first became apparent when she was at school; she had difficulty with reading, spelling and maths. After spending two years in Kenya, where her dad volunteered as a social worker, she returned to Minnesota and went to a private school. Ann thought that if she worked hard, then she could keep her difficulties a secret, or they might even go away – they didn't.

Ann was diagnosed with dyslexia. Her parents were pleased, but she wasn't. She didn't want to be different to the other kids. Ann's struggles meant that she was either pulled out of or discouraged from taking part in art, music and sports.

Alongside exploring, Ann's other passion is teaching. At university she studied physical education. Then, after four years working as a special education teacher, she was offered the opportunity of a lifetime to go to the North Pole.

Ann was the only woman on the expedition – even the 49 dogs who went with them were all male. In fact, she was the first woman ever to cross the ice and get to the North Pole. *Ms.* magazine named her woman of the year. When Ann had returned from the North Pole, she saw how excited the kids at her school were to hear about the mission. A few years later she started the Ann Bancroft Foundation (originally called the AWE Foundation), which supports girls to follow their dreams.

In 1993 Ann led the first all-women's expedition to the South Pole, making her the first woman in history to reach both the North and South Poles. She was becoming known all over the world, appearing on TV and in magazines and using her platform to raise awareness of important causes.

In 2001 Ann took part in possibly her most dangerous expedition yet: sailing and skiing across Antarctica with fellow explorer, Liv Arnessen. At that time of year the sun never sets in Antarctica, but that didn't mean it was warm – in fact, it was so cold that at one point Ann cried tears that froze inside her goggles. Some days they would walk for hours but only make it a few miles. The terrain was so dangerous that if things had gone wrong, they could have been left to die!

When Ann and Liv returned, they wrote and talked about the mission, inspiring young people all around the world. Ann told people that being dyslexic had helped her train for her expeditions because it taught her to work hard and take one step after the other.

It's hard to believe that Ann was once worried about being different. She's different to almost everyone else in the world. She's an explorer!

Discussion questions for your school, college or book club

→ Why do you think that Ann chooses to explore dangerous places?

→ Why do you think that Ann was unhappy when she received her dyslexia diagnosis?

→ What do you think made her change her mind and see it as an asset?

22
LAURA KATE DALE

Autistic Video Game Journalist with ADHD

Let's talk autistic special interests. It's common for autistic people to have a topic that they are very interested in. That's why if you ask me who my favourite rappers are (Biggie, Kendrick, Danny Brown), you may need to book an hour out for me to tell you everything I love about hip-hop. I am yet to find a way to monetize my special interest, but Laura Kate Dale, who has a special interest in video games, has managed to turn talking and writing about her special interest into a career.

Laura was introduced to video games at a young age by her older brother, who owned a Super Nintendo and an N64 (both early Nintendo consoles). When Laura was seven, an exciting new game came out called *Legend of Zelda: Ocarina of Time*. The game contained within it a whole world of stories and characters who interacted with each other – for Laura this felt magical! She struggled with socializing and there was something very reassuring about games where people would act in predictable ways.

A few years later, when the *Pokémon* games came out, Laura's video game interest evolved (yes, that pun was intentional) into an autistic special interest. It's hard to explain just how big of a deal *Pokémon* was in the late 1990s. There were about two or three years where, for school kids, everything revolved around *Pokémon*. We would get up, watch *Pokémon* cartoons on TV, go to school and swap *Pokémon* cards, then get home to spend the whole evening playing *Pokémon* video games. All social structures that existed before shifted and the most popular kid was now the one with a shiny Charizard card.

Pokémon hit all the things that Laura's brain liked: she could complete collections and learn about which levels specific *Pokémon* would evolve at or learn special moves. This helped

Laura make some friends, who found her in-depth *Pokémon* knowledge useful. The problem was that when the *Pokémon* phenomenon subsided and most children pursued other interests, Laura's interest stayed the same.

In Laura's words, she was 'the weird kid' in school. She spent lots of time alone, watching other children play. Sometimes she would eat her lunch in the bathroom to escape kids who made fun of her. She took things other children said very literally, and they used this to bully her, making her swap the good parts of her school lunch and tricking her into eating dirt. At secondary school, bullies stole her things, broke her stimming tools and told her that she was going to the wrong class because they knew that this made her anxious.

As she got older, Laura made some friendships based on things she was interested in: music, anime shows and, of course, video games. It was watching an anime show, recommended by a friend, that gave Laura the courage to come out as trans at aged 17. Although Laura had been assigned male at birth, she felt there was a distressing disconnect between her physical body and the way she viewed herself on a core personal level. Coming out was difficult, but as Laura began to present as female and be referred to as 'she' and 'her', she felt inherently more at home with herself.

Around this time Laura also received a diagnosis of Asperger's. When she was diagnosed, there was a lot of talk from doctors about things which she struggled with. She wasn't told that the different way that her brain worked could be turned into work. But over the coming years she would do just that.

In her 20s Laura worked long boring shifts in a supermarket while writing about video games in her spare time. She would keep a notebook with her at work and make notes when she had an idea for something to write about. She'd been writing for a video game conventions website and one day they started a magazine, which meant that they could pay Laura for her writing. It was a foot in the door to being a paid video games journalist. Her day job was boring and other staff members were transphobic, so Laura left the supermarket, giving herself a month to make it as a professional writer or else look for another job.

Fortunately, around this time a YouTuber called James Stephanie Sterling found Laura's work and invited her to work on a podcast with them. Laura grabbed this opportunity, which meant that she could talk about her special interest as a job.

Laura's now a successful video game journalist. Her interview with the game developer Peter Molyneux trended on Facebook and her unboxing of the PS4 Slim (which at the time hadn't even been announced) has over a million views on YouTube.

In 2019 Laura published *Uncomfortable Labels,* a book about her life as a gay, autistic, trans woman. In the book she talks about how she was so unhappy when she was younger that she prayed to God not to be autistic or trans, and to be happy in her own head. Her prayers not to be autistic or trans were not answered but her prayers to be happy in her own head were, in a roundabout way. In 2021 *Gender Euphoria* was published, a collection of writing from different trans, non-binary and intersex people curated by Laura (including some of her own stories). *Gender Euphoria* would focus on the joy that trans people had experienced from being true to themselves.

If Laura weren't autistic, then she wouldn't be the journalist she is today. Some of the work she is most proud of is when she leans into her neurodivergent traits, such as her quest to catch all the rare shiny variants in a *Pokémon* game, which took over 400 hours. She has also begun to talk about accessibility in video games, a topic that gets very little airtime. If there is an 'autistic dream', I think it is to turn a special interest into a career. I'm yet to put my hip-hop knowledge to good use, but Laura has turned her neurodivergent video game knowledge into a job she loves.

Discussion questions for your school, college or book club

→ What jobs might someone with an autistic special interest excel at because of that interest?

→ Laura dropped out of college but went on to be a successful writer. What can schools and colleges do to nurture neurodivergent talent?

→ What are the additional barriers faced by neurodivergent people who are also part of the LGBTQ+ community?

23

EMMA LEWELL-BUCK

Dyspraxic Politician

Wired Differently

Politics is one area of our lives where neurodivergent people are still incredibly underrepresented. But things are changing, with Jessica Benham being elected to the Pennsylvania House of Representatives in America and (closer to where I live) Emma Lewell-Buck representing South Shields in the UK Parliament.

South Shields is a coastal town in the north-east of England. It's where Emma grew up, as part of a working-class family that worked in the shipyard. At school it was clear she was different. She was always picked last in sports, and during her cycling proficiency test she was so bad that all the other children came to the window to watch her cycling straight over the cones. As a teenager, life wasn't any easier and she would always be the one to fall over with her tray in the school canteen. By the end of school, she was being punished for bad behaviour, which was her way of saying that she was struggling. Despite this, she was able to go to university to study politics and media.

Unlike many politicians who start out as political advisers before becoming members of parliament, Emma spent her early life doing any job that would pay the bills. She was a call centre worker, a shop assistant, bartender and more. Then, in her mid-20s, she decided to train as a social worker.

Emma went back to university for her training, and while she was there, on the suggestion of one of her lecturers, she went to see an educational psychologist, who diagnosed her with dyspraxia. Not knowing why she was different had knocked her confidence growing up, but now she would develop a completely different, more positive, outlook on her differently wired brain.

As a social worker, Emma saw poverty and injustice in her local community, which she wanted to do something about. In 2013 the MP for South Shields, David Miliband, decided to stand down as an MP (the reasons for this are complicated but very interesting – look them up!). This meant that there would have to be a by-election to decide who the new MP would be.

Emma was selected to fight the by-election as the Labour Party candidate. If she won, she would be the first female MP to hold the seat as well as the first person from the local area. Emma won the seat, by more than 6000 votes. In the elections that followed, even more people voted for her.

There are loads of potential reasons why an MP might increase the number of votes they get. However, Emma thinks that part of what makes her a good politician is her neurodivergence. Being dyspraxic means that she thinks differently to other people. When many politicians are going with the flow, and following a party line, someone who thinks outside the box is a rare commodity.

In 2017 Emma put forward a bill to parliament asking the government to measure food insecurity. Her thinking was that to stop people going hungry, we need to be able to measure it first. This way of thinking reminds me of lots of the other dyspraxic people I have spoken to or researched for this book, who break a problem down and in doing so find different ways of solving that problem. Two years later the government agreed to start measuring food insecurity.

This is not to say that life as an MP has been easy for Emma. Timekeeping during speeches can be difficult, especially in parliament when you can be told to cut down a speech while you're giving it. At her first party conference she tripped on a curb and fell over. People gathered round and Emma was worried that they would think she was drunk.

Despite these setbacks, Emma remains a proud dyspraxic person. In 2019 she helped launch Neurodivergent Labour, a group set up to speak up for neurodivergent people in her party and to think about how politics can help neurodivergent people everywhere.

I believe that having neurodivergent people in government is important but not just for the obvious reasons. Obviously, all jobs should be open to everyone and people should be supported and not discriminated against, but I think there's an even more important reason for the people running a country to be neurodiverse. The criticism of politicians I hear a lot is 'they're all the same', and to some extent I think that's fair: there aren't a lot of new ideas in politics. Emma is not 'the same' – she's neurodivergent. And I think in the future we will see lots more politicians who are different just like her.

Discussion activity for your school, college or book club

Form a fantasy government from neurodivergent people (either those listed in this book or others you know about). You will need someone to lead your government and a different person for each of the following departments (plus any others that you would like to create):

→ Education

→ Health

→ Arts and Culture

→ The Environment

→ Defence

→ Sport.

Discuss your reasons for assigning people to these positions.

24
ELLE McNICOLL

Autistic Writer

One in seven people is neurodivergent, which makes it odd that of the thousands of novels published every year only a few will have neurodivergent characters. When I do get to read a novel with one of us in, I often feel that something's not quite right. The character might tick all of the boxes for a diagnosis but they don't feel like the neurodivergent people I know in real life. It's a bit like when you buy supermarket own-brand versions of your favourite cereal; it's hard to say exactly what's wrong but it's just not the real thing.

Growing up, Elle McNicoll had these same frustrations. She wanted to read books about people like her but couldn't find any. So, when she was able to, she got a job in publishing, hoping that if she could be in the room where decisions about books were being made, then she could change things. Convincing publishers that neurodiversity was important was difficult. People thought that there wasn't a market for books with neurodivergent characters. Elle knew this wasn't true, so she wrote a book to prove them wrong. A small publisher who specialized in children's books written by people from diverse backgrounds agreed to print Elle's book and in 2020 *A Kind of Spark* was published. It sold out immediately.

A Kind of Spark is about a young autistic girl called Addie who campaigns to have a memorial in her small town for the women who were murdered after being falsely accused of witchcraft. Addie isn't like autistic characters I've met in other books. She feels like a real person; one who you really care about.

I was obviously not the only one who enjoyed *A Kind of Spark*. My social media feeds were full of people saying how great it was, and the reviews and awards kept coming in. Autistic adults like me had grown up looking for characters in books who were like us and we'd finally found one. Actually, we'd found two, because Addie's sister, Keedie, is also autistic. I'd never read a book with two neurodivergent characters! I guess when writers only have one idea of how an autistic character would act, there's no point in having more than one in a story.

Elle's follow-up, *Show Us Who You Are*, has more great neurodivergent characters but this time they're in a science fiction setting, navigating a creepy organization that is making holograms of dead people. The day my copy arrived in the post, Elle was on TV winning a Blue Peter Book Award for *A Kind of Spark* and proudly telling the world that she was a neurodivergent author.

What makes Elle's books so good? I think that as a neurodivergent writer she has a head start coming up with good neurodivergent characters. All authors draw on their own experiences when writing. They might not have been through the exact same things as their characters (otherwise fantasy novels would be *very* dangerous to write), but they try to put themselves in the minds of their characters to guess how they would behave. Elle's lived experience means that her neurodivergent characters act in a way that is so much more real than similar characters in other books. I believe that she is the start of a new age of great neurodivergent people telling incredible stories.

Discussion questions for your school, college or book club

→ Why is it important that the books we read reflect the neurodiversity of the world we live in?

→ What fictional neurodivergent characters can you think of from books, television or film?

→ Do these characters reflect the diversity of neurodivergent people you know and those in this book?

25
SAM HOLNESS
(AKA SUPER SAM)

Autistic Athlete

I trained with Sam Holness (also known as Super Sam) once as part of a TV show. He wore a T-shirt which had 'Autism is my superpower' on the front. After 30 minutes of trying to keep up with his warm-up routine (not even a proper training session), I was barely conscious, whereas Sam hadn't broken a sweat. I realized then that Sam truly does have a superpower. His autistic focus has completely transformed what his body is capable of, allowing him to compete internationally in intense athletic events.

Every superhero has an origin story and this is Sam's. Sam was diagnosed with autism at the age of four. At school, Sam didn't see it as a superpower; it meant that he struggled to communicate, and this made him feel frustrated. The teachers didn't recognize Sam's superpowers either.

One day, at secondary school, there was a swimming gala. When Sam put his hand up to say that he wanted to compete, the teachers didn't believe that Sam would be able to swim. In fact, Sam had been able to swim since before he could talk. When he was three years old, he was taken to a swimming pool for the first time. He learned to swim so quickly that after an hour he took off his armbands.

When he was 18, he started going to judo. He would always be the first to arrive at training and his sensei (judo teacher) nicknamed him 'Super Sam'. It took time for Sam to join in at judo and to learn to control how he moved, but eventually he became a fearless fighter and attained a brown belt (almost the highest-ranked belt).

The same year Sam joined a running club. It could be quite busy, which he didn't like, but the running helped Sam to regulate his breathing, reducing his anxiety. One day Sam saw online that there was a duathlon being held at the park near him (a duathlon is a race where people do part of the race on a bicycle and part on foot). He took part in his first duathlon, then shortly after that his first triathlon (like a duathlon but with swimming as well!).

It was around this time that Sam went to St Mary's University in London. On his induction day he saw the 400-metre track named after his favourite sportsperson, Mo Farah, who had trained there. Sam left university with a sports science degree. He wrote his dissertation on the ways in which sports coaches could better support autistic athletes by giving them respect and feedback, and having high aspirations for them.

Sam's own experiences with coaches weren't great. They would often speak too quickly and want to do sessions online, which Sam found difficult. Worst of all, they underestimated Sam because he was autistic. Sam's dad, Tony, took over as Sam's main coach. Unlike Sam's other coaches, Tony recognized that autism was Sam's superpower. Tony would help Sam to train six days a week and would travel abroad with him to compete in triathlons in countries such as Germany and Portugal.

In 2019 Sam and Tony were travelling for a triathlon. Tony got talking to the staff at a sportswear company called Hoka. The company were interested in Sam's story. He was unusual because not only was it rare for an autistic person to be competing at this level, but he was also the only black person taking part in this particular competition. By becoming an ambassador for Hoka, Sam showed that anyone can participate in sport and be a successful endurance athlete, no matter what their background.

Lots of people were starting to recognize Sam's superpower.

Magazines and TV shows wanted to talk to him and the Shaw Trust made him one of their top 100 people with a disability.

In 2020 the coronavirus pandemic meant that all of Sam's races were cancelled, but Sam kept training, doing open-water swimming when the pools were closed. At the time of writing, Sam is training hard, hoping to compete in the Ironman World Championships in Hawaii. This event involves a 3.8-kilometre swim, 180-kilometre cycle and a full-marathon run. Sam hopes to do this in under 11 hours!

People have underestimated Sam because he's autistic. But what those people don't realize is that autism is his superpower.

Discussion questions for your school, college or book club

→ How can schools do better to make sure that people like Sam are able to realize their superpowers earlier?

→ How can sport and exercise be more accessible for neurodivergent people?

→ In what ways does Sam's story challenge stereotypes of autistic people?

26
MICKEY ROWE

Autistic Actor

In recent years I've seen a lot of popular TV shows, film and theatre with neurodivergent characters in leading roles. A favourite of mine is the American TV show *Atypical*, which follows a young autistic boy, finding his way in the world – it was recently renewed for a fourth season. Here in the UK, *Doctor Who* featured a dyspraxic assistant, and more than 30 years ago the film *Rain Man* about an autistic adult was winning Oscars. It seems strange to me that neurodivergent characters are so often played by neurotypical actors. You would have thought that neurodivergent actors would be best placed to portray neurodivergent characters as they can draw on their real-life experiences. Lack of opportunity and barriers in the industry mean that more often than not neurodivergent roles end up going to neurotypical actors. I believe this will change and I believe that Mickey Rowe is the beginning of this change.

Mickey was the first autistic actor to play the lead role in the award-winning play *The Curious Incident of the Dog in the Night-Time* (I'm going to call it *Curious Incident* for the rest of the chapter because it's a very long title). Not only this but he was also one of the first autistic actors to play any autistic character, anywhere!

In high school, Mickey had no friends. He would spend lunch breaks pacing the hallway, not knowing whom to talk to or how to talk to them. It must have been a very lonely time. The only time he ever felt understood was sitting in the audience at the children's theatre his grandmother had a subscription to.

It's no surprise that, when Mickey was older, he studied drama at university. Not only had he spent all that time in the theatre, but he'd been an actor his whole life, pretending to be neurotypical when he wasn't. At university he received an autism diagnosis. One day, not long after that, a teacher gave him a monologue to read from the part of the autistic character in *Curious Incident*. Mickey wondered whether she knew that he was autistic.

Shortly afterwards, Mickey decided that he would stop pretending to be neurotypical. He wrote an essay for an industry website in which he talked about the challenges he had faced as someone both autistic and legally blind. He also talked about how being autistic had made him a better actor.

A couple of years later Mickey got to stand on stage and give the same monologue from *Curious Incident*, as part of the professional stage production at the Indiana Repertory Theatre in Indianapolis. There was a huge amount of press interest in Mickey's journey; *The New York Times*, Salon and CNN all ran stories on his casting.

Mickey has continued to speak up for autistic and disabled actors. He helped found the National Disability Theatre, an organization that aims to radically transform theatrical practices. He also writes about why representation of autistic people is important.

Mickey might have been the first openly autistic actor to play an autistic role, but he won't be the last. In 2021 it was announced that autistic actor Ashley Storrie would be playing the lead role in a British sitcom about a young autistic woman. I'm hopeful that in the future things will change and it will be normal for neurodivergent actors to play neurodivergent roles, and Mickey Rowe will go down in history as one of the people who made this change happen.

Discussion questions for your school, college or book club

→ Do you believe that it is important for neurodivergent roles to be played by neurodivergent actors? Why?

→ Why do you think that so many neurodivergent roles are played by neurotypical actors?

→ What are the barriers that neurodivergent actors face?

27
SIENA CASTELLON

Autistic, Dyspraxic and Dyslexic Activist and Writer

I have a theory that a school is the most neurodiverse place you can be. Most of the time the pupils who go there haven't chosen that school; it's just the closest one to where they happen to live. There are kids who get good grades and kids who get bad grades, kids who have lots of friends and kids who have none, kids who are quiet and kids who run around making lots of noise. It seems ridiculous to me that when schools are some of the most neurodiverse settings, they often don't recognize that diversity or properly support their neurodivergent students to achieve. Eighteen-year-old Siena Castellon is on a mission to change this.

School was very tough for Siena. She was bullied so much that she had to move schools multiple times. She knew that she was different; she didn't like loud sounds or bright lights, certain fabrics felt horrible and her vocabulary was very advanced for her age. It hadn't occurred to her that she could have been autistic; she had only seen the stereotypes of autism in the media and those stereotypes were all boys.

Growing up, Siena would watch TV shows, see how the characters would interact, and copy their body language and things they would say. Looking at her, people might have thought 'that person can't be autistic, they had a good conversation', but behind the scenes she was spending lots of time memorizing scripts and pretending to have a different personality.

At 12 Siena received an autism diagnosis. She says it felt like 'finally finding the elusive missing piece of a jigsaw puzzle'. It explained why she struggled to read body language and why she found social environments very draining. She had already been diagnosed with dyspraxia and dyslexia. The dyspraxia diagnosis had helped explain why she was often told that she wasn't trying at sport and with organization, even though she was putting a lot of effort in. The dyslexia diagnosis explained why Siena wrote her letters and numbers the wrong way around, skipped words when reading aloud and misspelled commonly used words.

Siena wasn't upset when she received her diagnoses. They didn't change anything about her; they just put a name to something which was already there. There were lots of positives too. Siena is incredibly passionate about maths, and part of that passion stems from her being autistic – she doesn't know who she'd be without that passion.

When Siena researched the conditions she had been diagnosed with online, she found information and resources targeted at parents but none for young people. Siena decided to start a website where young people could get practical advice on how to overcome some of the challenges that young neurodivergent people face. The website was called Quantum Leap Mentoring and it became hugely popular.

From the outside it might seem like Siena's life from here was back-to-back success. But at school bullies (one of whom used to be her best friend) began trying to trick her and making up lies about Siena, forcing her to leave another school. Siena had already moved schools twice because of bullying; this time she wrote about her experiences on her website alongside practical tips on how to deal with bullying. She would soon be chosen out of thousands of applicants to sit on the National Anti-Bullying Youth Board, run by the Diana Award's Anti-Bullying Campaign.

Awards were coming in all the time for Siena – one was given to her by the Prime Minister and another meant she was invited to

Kensington Palace to meet royalty. People in the media also heard about Siena and invited her on to TV and radio shows to talk about why neurodiversity was important. In 2018 she was given a Teen Hero Award by BBC Radio 1, appearing onstage in front of 10,000 other teenagers.

Siena was often contacted by young neurodivergent people who would tell her that they were using the tips on her website. Some of them said that they weren't getting very far because teachers weren't listening to them. She came up with a solution – Neurodiversity Celebration Week. This would be a week every year where schools, colleges and universities from all around the world would sign up to take part in different ways. The week aimed to teach teachers more about neurodiversity, to educate neurotypical students and to empower neurodivergent individuals. As I write this, there are more than 1500 schools signed up to take part in Neurodiversity Celebration Week, which means the event is reaching over 900,000 young people.

Siena's next project was a book called *The Spectrum Girl's Survival Guide: How to Grow Up Awesome and Autistic*. It was the first book written for autistic girls by an autistic girl. The book covers everything from social exhaustion to skincare routines. In 2020 Siena successfully raised £2000 so that a copy of the book could be sent to every state girls' school in the UK. The follow-up to that book came out a year later; this time Siena had created a workbook especially for autistic girls.

I think it's important to say that, as I write this, Siena is just 18 years old! Already she has two books published, multiple awards, a campaign reaching close to a million young people – incredible achievements for someone of any age. By speaking out about her negative experiences of a school system that doesn't recognize neurodiversity and being a proud neurodivergent person, she is changing the world for the better.

Discussion questions for your school, college or book club

→ What can schools and colleges do to prevent bullying of neurodivergent pupils?

→ What are the most important things for teachers to know about neurodiversity?

→ Is it important that young neurodivergent people are involved in creating resources about neurodivergent conditions? If so, why?

28
SUZI RUFFELL

Dyslexic Comedian

This is probably an autistic trait, but sometimes I will find a word or phrase I like and become a bit fixated on it. As I write this, the phrase is 'writing on my own terms'. Comedian Suzi Ruffell said that was what she did in a newspaper article in 2018 and I think its brilliant. I like the idea that writers should set the terms that they write on (if you're wondering, my terms are no background noise, Earl Grey tea and an unhealthy amount of biscuits).

At school, neurodivergent people can often struggle with writing. Not because we're bad writers but because schools have a very specific way that they expect people to write – one that works a lot better for neurotypical people. I think sometimes neurodivergent people don't realize how creative they are because they've never had a chance to do things on their own terms.

Born in 1986, Suzi comes from a long line of storytellers. Her dad and her uncle always had brilliant anecdotes to tell (always told, never written down). Suzi carried on this family tradition. At school her head was buzzing with ideas and stories to tell, but when it came to writing those ideas down, they never came out how she wanted them to. She found every lesson where she needed to read or write difficult – and that was most of them. She lived for Thursday evenings when she would go to her local drama group, where creativity and storytelling were celebrated.

As a teenager, Suzi was diagnosed with dyslexia, which she was told was quite common for creative people. She thought that was pretty cool, like she was part of a special creative club. She worked hard and had support from her school so she could pass her exams and go to drama school.

After graduating from drama school, Suzi worked as an actor

alongside other jobs for a few years, then she booked in her first stand-up comedy gig. It was in a room above a pub. There were eight people in the audience (well, seven people and a dog). There wasn't a stage, the lighting was bad and the microphone kept cutting out. Despite all this, when Suzi got a few laughs from the audience, she knew that this was what she wanted to do.

Suzi started doing more stand-up comedy and watching other comedians, too. She signed to a big agent who also represented her favourite comedian – Alan Carr. Her agents sent her to comedy clubs all around the country, performing to crowds much bigger than seven people and a dog. Soon she was getting spots on TV and taking solo shows to the Edinburgh Fringe Festival.

In 2015, Suzi was booked for her dream gig – going on tour as Alan Carr's support act. She saw how excited Alan's fans were to meet him after the shows, treating him as if he were their friend. Every night Alan's show would be slightly different. He wasn't like other comedians who had an exact script he stuck to; he used the words that felt right on the night. This made his act feel more like a chat with a very funny friend than a speech, which was probably why the audience were so pleased to meet him afterwards. Suzi was so inspired by Alan: he wasn't like the other comedians – he was doing things on his own terms.

Suzi decided to write a new solo show, but this time she would do it differently. For her old shows she had used a laptop to write out what she would say word for word. Now she started to go out on stage with just a few notes to remind her of ideas she wanted to talk about. She was writing, but not in the way that she was taught at school. She knew that no one would be marking her notes, so it didn't matter what they looked like; it only mattered what they sounded like when she went out on stage and told those stories.

Suzi also decided that she would talk about the things that were important to her, especially her family – after all, that was where she got her passion for storytelling from. Suzi came from a working-class family, and a lot of the other comedians she knew came from middle-class families – their families did different jobs, had more money and sent their children to private schools. In comedy it's always a good thing to be different to other comedians, so by talking about her background Suzi would stand out from the crowd.

The show was called *Common* (British slang for working-class) and it was a hit! Suzi started to appear all over TV and radio and was thought of as a great writer. Newspapers would get in touch and ask her to write articles (which she would get her girlfriend to proofread before she sent off). Before *Common*, she was thinking about giving up, and just over two years later she was booked to appear on *Live at the Apollo* – the biggest stand-up show in the UK – with material she had never written down in full.

Suzi's comedy is all about being proud of who you are. As a working-class, neurodivergent lesbian, there were lots of people telling her not to be proud, but she doesn't listen to any of them. Right now Suzi is booked to return to her home town to perform at one of the biggest theatres in the city, and it's all because she decided to write on her own terms.

Discussion questions for your school, college or book club

→ If you were in charge of a school, what changes would you make so that neurodivergent young people could write on their own terms?

→ What would a lesson in your school look like?

→ What would a pupil have to do to get an A grade in your school?

29
JON ADAMS

Autistic and Dyslexic Artist

I think that one of the biggest barriers neurodivergent people face is the low expectations of neurotypical people. Sometimes when you get told that you're useless, you start to believe it yourself. When Jon Adams was at school, a teacher tore up a piece of his work in front of the whole class, telling him that he would 'never be anything'.

Today it's hard to think of anything Jon isn't! He's an artist, an activist, a playwright, a geologist, an advocate, a scientific illustrator and a poet. He calls himself a 'pesky autistic person' because he can't keep quiet when neurodivergent people are being mistreated or excluded, which makes him 'pesky' for those people who find it easier to just ignore it. Jon doesn't just think differently; he demands that other people think differently too, through his art and his activism.

Growing up in the 1960s and 1970s, Jon's childhood was different to that of most young people growing up today. The school system Jon went through was unimaginably hostile to neurodivergent pupils. In junior school, Jon was put in the 'retarded readers' class (an offensive term, thankfully not used by schools anymore) and at secondary school he was treated even worse. When he spoke, he could explain things very well (especially science and anything about the natural world) but he found it difficult to put his ideas into writing. This meant that he was labelled lazy for not writing enough and a swot for knowing all the answers. The teachers bullied Jon, and the incident where his teacher said Jon would 'never be anything' after he spelled his name wrong on one of his (excellent) drawings led to Jon developing post-traumatic stress disorder, a type of mental illness caused by a traumatic event, sometimes shortened to PTSD.

Not everything was bad at school; Jon had a best friend (who it turns out was also autistic), and his differently wired brain allowed him to come up with great pranks he could play on the teachers. For example, hiding an alarm clock in another kid's bag, set to go off ten minutes before the end of the day, so that the teacher would think it was the school bell and let them out early – it actually worked!

Thinking differently also earned Jon a place at university. For his entrance interview, the professor asked him, 'How deep is the Solent?' The Solent is a stretch of water between the Isle of Wight and the south coast of England. According to Google, the answer is 46 metres, but Jon replied, 'It depends where you measure it?' Jon was right: at the edge of the Solent it's just a few centimetres deep – it's only 46 metres deep in the middle. The professor liked how Jon thought about the question differently to other people interviewed and gave him a place to study geology.

Jon always knew he was different. At school he learned that being different would see him humiliated, punished and bullied. But he also learned that thinking differently was what made him great. After leaving university, Jon worked as a scientific illustrator (the perfect job because he was good at drawing and science) before deciding to start making his own artwork.

Jon has made all different types of art, and I love all of it. His drawings of vulture-like birds representing PTSD are terrifying, his poems about mental health are powerful and his short plays are hilarious!

Jon's conceptual pieces are my favourite. These are the art pieces that focus on an interesting idea, designed to make people think.

There was one where he sat in central London in a hazmat suit and used a scalpel to remove the word 'spelling' from dictionaries. Another had a locked bookshelf which could only be unlocked using a spanner attached to a chain that was too short to reach. My favourite Jon Adams piece had remained a secret until I spoke to him during my research for this book. He went to a gallery in Chichester with lots of little pieces of paper with the word 'swept' on them. He went into a room which he knew had a big rug on the floor and, when no one was looking, he put them under it ('swept under the rug' – get it?). He then left without telling anyone what he'd done. If you're ever in the Pallant House Gallery in Chichester and you see a rug, then do lift up the corner to see if Jon's 'swepts' are still there.

It wasn't until he was almost 40 that Jon discovered that he was neurodivergent. When he did, he recognized how poorly he had been treated because of his differences and how misunderstood neurodivergent people were. Jon felt a responsibility to make sure that the next generation of neurodivergent young people didn't have to go through the same things he had been through.

Not afraid of authority, Jon used his position as an artist to talk to powerful people, including politicians, journalists and important academics. Jon even founded a charity called Flow Observatorium, which works to make sure that neurodivergent people aren't left out of the arts world. Jon has spent the latter part of his life sharing his simple message with anyone who would listen: that neurodivergent people should be treated with respect, included and supported to reach their full potential without changing who they are.

Jon's activism has a ripple effect. It inspires the people around him and then they go out and inspire the people around them. His passion for justice is infectious and it's spreading around the world. Not bad for someone who was told he would never be anything.

Discussion questions for your school, college or book club

→ What effect do you think it had on Jon being told that he would never be anything?

→ Do you think that people's expectations of what neurodivergent people can achieve has improved since the time when Jon was growing up?

→ How can you change your school, college or workplace so that neurodivergent people believe that they can be anything?

30
SIMONE BILES

Gymnast with ADHD

Everyone in this book is great but Simone Biles is the GOAT (*the* GOAT means the Greatest Of All Time, not to be confused with *a* goat, which is an animal). She has won more world championship medals than any other gymnast in history, as well as multiple Olympic gold medals, and she has even had a gymnastics move named after her.

Simone was born in 1997 in Ohio, with an older sister and brother. Two years later her younger sister Adria was born. Life was tough. Her birth mother, Shannon, struggled with addiction and found it difficult to look after Simone and her siblings. Sometimes they had to eat cereal with water because there was no milk in the house. Neighbours noticed that Simone and her siblings were playing on their own most of the time so they called social services. A social worker visited the family and decided that the children should be taken into foster care.

After a few months with a foster family, Simone's grandparents came to visit and told her that they would be looking after Simone, her brother and her sisters, while Shannon got better. Sadly, Shannon continued to struggle with addiction, so in 2003 Simone's grandparents adopted her and her siblings and became known to Simone as Mom and Dad.

Simone loved her new home, in part because it had a trampoline – her foster home had one too but she wasn't allowed to use it. Simone would spend hours playing on it, doing twirls and flips.

In 2003 Simone's day care took a trip to Bannon's Gym. Simone took to the trampoline and copied some of the moves that the older gymnasts were doing (they weren't that different from the moves she'd taught herself on the trampoline at home). Her older brother, who was working at the day care, dared Simone to do a backflip. So she did. Perfectly. At this point, Veronica, a woman who worked at the gym, came over and asked Simone's brother if she had been trained to do gymnastics. Veronica couldn't believe that someone as young as Simone and with no training could be so good.

Veronica knew that Simone had something special, so she assigned her daughter, Aimee, to train her. With Aimee's help, she quickly rose up the levels and was heading towards competing at a national level, with Simone quickly outperforming even Aimee.

Everyone could see that there was something different about Simone. For a start she was much more muscular than the other children at school, but she was also full of energy, ALL the time. In the gym she could focus that energy into her training, but at school the slightest thing would distract her from her work. In 2011 her dad decided to have her assessed for ADHD, and no one was surprised when she received the diagnosis. She began taking medication to help her to concentrate at school.

In 2013 Simone was chosen to compete in the American Cup, her first national competition, and the first to be broadcast on television. All eyes were on Simone and the pressure got the better of her; she fell from the bars, she wobbled on the beam and she even hurt her ankle on the floor. Everyone knew she could do the moves, even Simone, but under the pressure of a national competition, she was distracted, worrying about what everyone was thinking. Gymnastics had got serious, and Simone wasn't having as much fun as she used to have.

She went to see a sports psychologist, who helped her to enjoy gymnastics again, just in time for her first international competition later that year. The World Artistic Gymnastics Championships in Belgium saw Simone win a gold medal. She also performed a move that no one had ever seen before in a competition. The move consisted of a double flip and a half twist, and it would come to be known as 'The Biles'. Simone had left her mark on the history of gymnastics.

The next few years would see Simone winning more competitions and pushing back against incredible adversity. A media storm brewed after Simone was the victim of racist comments from another gymnast and her trainer. If that wasn't enough to deal with, Simone also needed to have surgery on her ankle, recover from an injured shoulder and find a new place to train. Simone persevered and won gold medals in the US Classic competition and the US National Gymnastics Championships, before going to China to become the world champion in the all-around competition for the second year in a row.

2016 was the year that Simone had been waiting for her whole life: the Rio de Janeiro Olympics. Simone was chosen to be on the team of five women to compete for the US. She won FOUR gold medals, setting an American record and proving that she was one of the most important gymnasts in Olympic history.

A month after winning those medals, computer hackers released the medical information of several Olympic athletes. They shared that Simone was taking medication that helped her concentrate in school. Simone didn't have to discuss her private medical information but she thought it was important to let everyone know that she wasn't ashamed of having ADHD, so she took to social media to tell the world. She would go on to be a proud neurodivergent person and has said that ADHD was a 'superpower', which means a lot coming from someone with four Olympic gold medals.

Over the next few years Simone would cement her title as the Greatest Of All Time, winning titles around the world, speaking out against injustice and setting up a fund to help pay for the cost of education for young people growing up in foster care. She even wore a custom-made leotard with her name and a picture of a goat on it, to make sure there wasn't any doubt.

At the 2021 Olympics, Simone withdrew from some events to focus on her mental health (while still winning two medals for the US). She was criticized in parts of the media, but out in the real world she gained even more fans, who admired her bravery in being so open and showing that even the GOAT must look after her mental health.

There's something exciting about knowing that truly great people are neurodivergent. When they're on TV, we can point to them and say, 'That's one of us!' It's even more exciting to know that the Greatest Of All Time is one of us – that there isn't a limit to what neurodivergent people can achieve. Not all neurodivergent people can be the GOAT – that position has been taken – but Simone's message of hard work, pride and resilience is one that we can all use to become the Greatest Version Of Ourselves (or GVOO for short).

Discussion questions for your school, college or book club

→ What is Simone's most important achievement?

→ What do you think the greatest version of you would be like?

→ What makes someone 'great'?

GOODBYE

And that's 30!

A few people have asked me what the criteria are for including people in this book. I've picked people whom I find interesting, who have done cool things and who are important in recent neurodivergent history. Much like when people ask me what my favourite albums are, there are so many I like that my list of favourites is always changing. If you bump into me after reading this book, then I'll probably tell you about all the new, exciting, neurodivergent people I've been learning about.

When I agreed to write this book, I didn't realize how much responsibility I would feel telling other people's stories. Especially when so many people in this book have told their own stories in such unique and powerful ways, retelling those stories has sometimes felt like trying to perform a complicated piece of classical music using instruments I've found in a toy box. I'd urge you all to go out and read Donna Williams, listen to Loyle Carner and get tickets for Hannah Gadsby (if you can!).

One of the main things I've learned from the time I've spent reading, listening and talking to neurodivergent people for this book is that all neurodivergent people are different. They look different, sound different, taste different and smell different (not actually sure about those last two – my research hasn't been *that* extensive). Neurodivergent people exist all over the world and in every class, gender, race and sexuality. On other planets there are probably neurodivergent aliens too (again, my research hasn't gone far enough to say if neurodiversity exists in outer space). This is why proper meaningful representation is important. We can't just hear one neurodivergent person's story and go, 'Well, we've told that story' – we need to hear lots of neurodivergent stories about different neurodivergent people. I hope that you use this book as a jumping-off point to hear more neurodivergent stories being told in different ways.

Another big thing I've learned is that there are neurodivergent experiences that cut across all cultures and backgrounds. In the stories of the people in this book, I recognized experiences I'd had in every one, even though some of the people came from completely different backgrounds. I was lucky enough to interview some of the people I wrote about in the book. After I'd done a couple of interviews, I had to put a post-it note on my laptop reminding me not to say 'Me too!' because I kept interrupting them to say that I'd had the same experience or felt the same way. Stories of bullying, being misunderstood by the school system and painful masking came up over and over again. But also joyful experiences of being understood and of learning to love the way your brain is wired. I've learned that these experiences can connect neurodivergent people all around the world.

Some of my favourite stories to hear about were of neurodivergent people meeting other neurodivergent people for the first time. Like when Warren Fried met fellow dyspraxic Mary Colley, or when dyslexic children excitedly get to meet Benjamin Zephaniah. It's increasingly easy for neurodivergent people to connect with our fellow neurodivergents. People are talking more and more about 'the neurodivergent community' or, as I once saw someone on Twitter call it, the 'neurosquad' (which I liked because it made us sound like a crime-fighting team).

My prediction is that neurodivergent people meeting in person or online to share experiences will be the thing that helps bring about change. We will speak out as a group when neurodivergent people are being mistreated or stopped from reaching their full potential. Together we will change the world.

I've got to include a few apologies in this final chapter. The first one is for anyone reading this book in the future and saying, 'I can't believe he used *that* term in a book'. The way we talk about neurodiversity is changing all the time; if you read any book about the topic more than ten years old, then you'll probably find language which feels really outdated. If the books written ten years ago use dated language, then this book will probably feel dated in the future. What's exciting about neurodiversity is that we're still working stuff out, and part of that working out is coming up with the language to talk about it.

My second apology is to everyone thinking, 'I can't believe he didn't include this person!' There are so many great neurodivergent people whom I didn't find space for. Robin Jax is an autistic musician who founded Tiergarten Records, a ground-breaking neurodiverse record label which puts out music made by neurodivergent artists from all backgrounds. While I'm talking about music, PKN are a Finnish punk band with learning disabled members. The boxer and civil rights activist, Muhammad Ali, was dyslexic and worked to improve literacy for African Americans. Comedian Andrew O'Neill has ADHD and their unique way of thinking oozes out of their original comedy style. If I'd had space, I would have written about all of these people and more.

I've also missed out a lot of historical figures who were believed to be neurodivergent. It can be hard to tell if someone who died a long time ago was neurodivergent, but it's often said that Alan Turing, who cracked the Enigma code and helped bring an end to the Second World War, was autistic. Turing would go on to be persecuted for being gay, was chemically castrated by the state and died tragically not long after. Another great scientist, Henry Cavendish, would take the same walk at the same time every night and eat the same meal every day. His focus on his work would lead him to discover hydrogen. It is hard to imagine that he was neurotypical.

The other people I've missed out of this book are the millions of neurodivergent people who aren't public figures but who make mine and other people's lives better in every way possible. The idea that you have to achieve something 'great' to be worth anything is rubbish. The neurodivergent people who are most important to me aren't the ones in this book; they're my friends and colleagues who make my life worth living. Neurodivergent friends are great. I have some neurodivergent friends who will always tell me the truth (even when I don't want to hear it) and others whose company I could spend hours in without ever getting bored.

One word I've tried to avoid using in this book is 'inspiring'. I find that neurodivergent people are always called this just for existing. It's as though some neurotypical people think, 'Blimey, if I were like that, I'd just give up. Well done them!'

You'll notice, however, that I have failed in my attempt not to use the word 'inspiring', but I've only used it when people are genuinely inspiring. Siena Castellon has inspired schools to celebrate neurodiversity, Naoki Higashida has inspired people to think differently about people who don't speak and Dara McAnulty's book did inspire me to appreciate the natural world around me.

I suppose I'm going to have to embrace the word 'inspiring'. The people in this book are inspiring, not just for being neurodivergent, but because of the effect that their work has on people. They have done (or are doing) things that inspire others to think differently, act differently, create differently and change the world.

Here's my parting challenge to you. Think about who in this book has inspired you. Not in an 'Ooh, aren't they inspiring!' way, but in a meaningful way, where they inspire you to think differently, act differently or do something new.

Write their name down here

. . . .

Now write down what they have inspired you to do

. . . .

. . . .

Close the book, go out and do it!

Acknowledgements

Thank you to Ruby Jewell for her helpful feedback on the first draft, to Jake Young for proofreading my early drafts and to Andrew Brenner for his invaluable advice and expertise.

References

Introduction

ACAS (2019) 'Neurodiversity at work.' Accessed on 13/9/2021 at https://archive.acas.org.uk/neurodiversity.

Forbes (n.d.) 'Jay-Z: Real time net worth.' Accessed on 13/9/2021 at www.forbes.com/profile/jay-z/#716b8a3359cf.

MarketResearch.com (n.d.) 'The U.S. Market For Autism Treatment.' Accessed on 13/9/2021 at www.marketresearch.com/Marketdata-Enterprises-Inc-v416/Autism-Treatment-11905455/?progid=90513.

Rose, B. (2016) 'The relief and grief of a child being diagnosed with autism.' BBC News. Accessed on 13/9/2021 at www.bbc.co.uk/news/disability-35820081.

Thunberg, G. (2019) 'When haters go after your looks and differences, it means they have nowhere left to go. And then you know you're winning! I have Aspergers and that means I'm sometimes a bit different from the norm. And – given the right circumstances – being different is a superpower. #aspiepower.' Tweet. Accessed on 13/9/2021 at https://twitter.com/GretaThunberg/status/1167916177927991296.

Greta Thunberg

Autistic UK CIC (n.d.) 'Neurodiversity.' Accessed on 13/9/2021 at https://autisticuk.org/neurodiversity.

CBS Mornings (2019) 'Greta Thunberg on the "gift" of Asperger's in fighting climate change: "We need people who think..."' YouTube. Accessed on 13/9/2021 at www.youtube.com/watch?v=BQ4rBLCpEeM&t=237s.

References

Global Climate Change: Vital Signs of the Planet (2013) 'Do scientists agree on climate change?' Accessed on 13/9/2021 at https://climate.nasa.gov/faq/17/do-scientists-agree-on-climate-change.

Reuters (2019) 'Greta Thunberg reaches New York after two-week sailing journey across Atlantic – video.' *The Guardian*, 29 August. Accessed on 13/9/2021 at www.theguardian.com/environment/video/2019/aug/29/greta-thunberg-reaches-new-york-after-two-week-sailing-journey-across-atlantic-video.

Taylor, M. (2018) '15 environmental protesters arrested at civil disobedience campaign in London.' *The Guardian*, 31 October. Accessed on 13/9/2021 at www.theguardian.com/environment/2018/oct/31/15-environmental-protesters-arrested-at-civil-disobedience-campaign-in-london.

Thunberg, G. (2019) *No One Is Too Small to Make a Difference*. London: Penguin/Random House.

Michael Buckholtz

AVA (2009) 'Michael Buckholtz hunger strike updates.' Action for Autism. Accessed on 13/9/2021 at http://actionforautism.blogspot.com/2009/05/michael-buckholtz-on-hunger-strike-for.html.

Buckholtz, M. (2021) Wired Differently research interview with Michael Buckholtz, 18 January.

GuideStar (n.d.) 'Aid for Autistic Children Foundation Incorporated – GuideStar Profile.' Accessed on 13/9/2021 at www.guidestar.org/profile/26-0707850.

Official Hot Mike (n.d.) 'The story.' Accessed on 13/9/2021 at https://officialhotmike.com/sample-page/his-story.

Warren Fried

Dyspraxia Foundation (n.d.) 'Warren Fried's Story.' Accessed on 13/9/2021 at https://dyspraxiausa.org/stories/warren-frieds-story.

Fried, W. (2020) 'Interview with Founder of Dyspraxia USA, Warren Fried.' JKP Blog. Accessed on 13/9/2021 at https://blog.jkp.com/2020/03/founder-of-dyspraxia-usa-warren-fried.

Fried, W. (2020) Wired Differently research interview with Warren Fried, 15 September.

Rubin, B.M. (2006) 'One man's passion: To spotlight dyspraxia.' *Chicago Tribune*, 6 September. Accessed on 13/9/2021 at www.chicagotribune. com/news/ct-xpm-2006-09-06-0609060183-story.html.

Fahima Abdulrahman

Abdulrahman, F. (2018) 'This Syrian man has been stuck in an airport for months.' BBC News, 9 July. Accessed on 13/9/2021 at www.bbc.co.uk/ news/av/stories-44738942.

Abdulrahman, F. (2019) 'Bumi Thomas: British-born jazz artist faces deportation from the UK.' BBC News, 1 August. Accessed on 13/9/2021 at www.bbc.co.uk/news/av/uk-49065905.

Abdulrahman, F. (2019) 'The mayor who wears a hijab.' BBC News, 25 May. Accessed on 13/9/2021 at www.bbc.co.uk/news/av/uk-politics-48401923.

Abdulrahman, F. (2020) Wired Differently research interview with Fahima Abdulrahman, 19 October.

BBC Trending (2017) 'Flying without a man: The mysterious case of Dina Ali.' BBC News, 1 June. Accessed on 13/9/2021 at www.bbc.co.uk/news/ blogs-trending-40105983.

LaCapria, K. (2017) 'Save Dina Ali.' Snopes, 12 April. Accessed on 13/9/2021 at www.snopes.com/news/2017/04/12/save-dina-ali-lasloom.

Van Wagtendonk, A. (2019) 'Saudi Arabia changed its guardianship laws, but activists who fought them remain imprisoned.' Vox, 3 August. Accessed on 13/9/2021 at www.vox.com/world/2019/8/3/20752864/saudi-arabia-guardianship-laws-women-travel-employment-mbs.

Pip Jamieson

Carroll, H. (2020) 'We turned our soul-crushing struggles into our superpowers: ADHD. Dyslexia. Autism. Meet the women proving these conditions are no longer an obstacle to success — but their secret weapons.' Mail Online, 8 June. Accessed on 13/9/2021 at www.dailymail.

co.uk/femail/article-8396763/We-turned-soul-crushing-struggles-superpowers.html.

CreativeMornings (2013) 'Pip Jamieson: The Loop.' CreativeMornings/SYD, 25 January. Accessed on 13/9/2021 at https://creativemornings.com/talks/pip-jamieson.

Fair Play Talks (2020) '50% employers admit they won't hire neurodivergent talent.' Fair Play Talks, 3 November. Accessed on 13/9/2021 at www.fairplaytalks.com/2020/11/03/50-employers-admit-they-wont-hire-neurodivergent-talent-reveals-ilm-study.

GMB Union (2018) 'Neurodiversity in the workplace: Thinking differently at work – Toolkit.' Accessed on 13/9/2021 at www.gmb.org.uk/sites/default/files/neurodiversity_workplace_toolkit.pdf.

Lawson, A. (2018) 'Entrepreneurs: The Dots founder behind LinkedIn rival for creatives.' *Evening Standard*, 5 February. Accessed on 13/9/2021 at www.standard.co.uk/business/entrepreneurs-the-dots-founder-behind-linkedin-rival-for-no-collar-creatives-a3758081.html#r3z-addoor.

Racovolis, K. (2016) 'The next LinkedIn? This woman is connecting 1 million creatives to jobs.' *Forbes*, 18 July. Accessed on 13/9/2021 at www.forbes.com/sites/kateracovolis/2016/07/18/the-next-linkedin-this-woman-is-connecting-1-million-creatives-to-jobs/?sh=84f6a85100f7.

The Loop (n.d.) 'Join The Loop. Australia's Creative Community.' Accessed on 13/9/2021 at www.theloop.com.au.

Jessica Thom

Caird, J. (2014) 'Jess Thom AKA Touretteshero: Comedy at its most unpredictable.' *The Guardian*, 9 July. Accessed on 13/9/2021 at www.theguardian.com/culture/2014/jul/09/jess-thom-tourettes-hero-comedy.

Donaldson James, S. (2012) 'Woman with Tourette's says 'biscuit' 16,000 times a day.' ABC News, 28 September. Accessed on 13/9/2021 at https://abcnews.go.com/Health/tourettes-syndrome-woman-biscuit-16000-times-day/story?id=17344295.

Foundation for People with Learning Disabilities (n.d.) 'Social model of

disability.' Accessed on 13/9/2021 at www.learningdisabilities.org.uk/
learning-disabilities/a-to-z/s/social-model-disability.

Howard, R. (2015) 'Russell speaks to real life hero Jess Thom.' YouTube.
Accessed on 13/9/2021 at www.youtube.com/watch?v=i8gOcbneQRQ.

TEDx Talks (2013) 'Tourette's syndrome – why it doesn't define me.'
YouTube. Accessed on 13/9/2021 at www.youtube.com/watch?v=_
jmTlQld2Z8.

Thom, J. (2012) *Welcome to Biscuit Land : A Year in the Life of
Touretteshero*. London: Souvenir Press.

Thom, J. (2021) Wired Differently research interview with Jessica Thom, 28
April.

Farah Nanji (aka DJ Ninja)

DJ-Ninja (n.d.) 'About.' Accessed on 13/9/2021 at www.dj-ninja.com/about.

Nanji, F. (2021) Wired Differently research interview with Farah Nanji, 3
February.

Speaker Associates (n.d.) 'Farah Nanji: Biography highlights.' Accessed on
13/9/2021 at www.speakersassociates.com/speaker/farah-nanji.

TEDx Talks (2019) 'Rewiring dyspraxia from the brain | Farah Nanji |
TEDxLuxembourgCity.' YouTube. Accessed on 13/9/2021 at www.
youtube.com/watch?v=OoT1MKh2JiM&t=356s.

Naoki Higashida

Higashida, N., Yoshida, K. and Mitchell, D. (2014) *The Reason I Jump: One
Boy's Voice from the Silence of Autism*. London: Sceptre.

Higashida, N., Mitchell, D. and Yoshida, K. (2018) *Fall Down 7 Times, Get Up
8: A Young Man's Voice from the Silence of Autism*. London: Sceptre.

Kinchen, R. (2013) 'Japanese teenager unable to speak writes autism
bestseller.' *The Sunday Times*, 14 July. Accessed on 13/9/2021 at www.
thetimes.co.uk/article/japanese-teenager-unable-to-speak-writes-
autism-bestseller-g5hwhhsoskd.

Mukhopadhyay, T.R. (2015) *Plankton Dreams: What I Learned in Special Ed*.
London: Open Humanities Press.

References

Spectra Blog (2017) 'Autistic badges; no more 'high-functioning' or 'low-functioning' labels for autism.' Accessed on 13/9/2021 at https://spectra. blog/news-views/autistic-badges-do-we-need-high-functioning-or-low-functioning-labels-for-autism.

Waterstones (2013) 'David Mitchell discusses *The Reason I Jump* by Naoki Higashida.' YouTube. Accessed on 13/9/2021 at www.youtube.com/watch?v=4YIoPRs9pq.

Wurzburg, G. (2015) Wretches & Jabberers [on demand]. Vimeo. Accessed on 13/9/2021 at https://vimeo.com/ondemand/wretchesjabberers?autoplay=1.

Benjamin Zephaniah

British Council (n.d.) 'Benjamin Zephaniah: Biography.' Accessed on 13/9/2021 at https://literature.britishcouncil.org/writer/benjamin-zephaniah.

Zephaniah, B. (2018) *The Life and Rhymes of Benjamin Zephaniah: The Autobiography*. London: Scribner.

Zephaniah, B. (2021) Wired Differently research interview with Benjamin Zephaniah, 8 January.

Lydia X.Z. Brown

Brown, L.X.Z. (2021) Wired Differently research interview with Lydia X.Z. Brown, 21 May.

Brown, L.X.Z., Ashkenazy, E. and Onaiwu, M.G. (eds) (2017) *All the Weight of Our Dreams: On Living Racialized Autism*. Lincoln, NE: Dragonbee Press, an imprint of the Autism Women's Network.

Change.org. (n.d.) 'End abuse of autistic students in Mercy County, Kentucky' [petition]. Accessed on 13/9/2021 at www.change.org/p/end-abuse-of-autistic-students-in-mercer-county-kentucky.

MassLive (2020) 'After FDA bans Massachusetts school from using electric shock devices, advocates seek public apology, reparations.' News, 9 March. Accessed on 13/9/2021 at https://www.masslive.com/news/2020/03/after-fda-bans-judge-rotenberg-center-from-using-

electric-shock-devices-advocates-seek-public-apology-reparations.
html.

Quallen, M. (2015) 'QUALLEN: For disabled students, the struggle
continues.' The Hoya, 26 February. Accessed on 13/9/2021 at https://
thehoya.com/disabled-students-struggle-continues.

The Georgetown Voice (n.d.) 'Lydia Brown, author at *The Georgetown
Voice*.' Accessed on 13/9/2021 at https://georgetownvoice.com/author/
lydia-brown.

Samantha Stein (aka Yo Samdy Sam)

Stein, S. (2020) Wired Differently research interview with Samantha Stein, 2
November.

YouTube (n.d.) 'Yo Samdy Sam' [YouTube channel]. Accessed on 13/9/2021
at https://www.youtube.com/c/YoSamdySam/featured.

Yo Samdy Sam (2019) 'Diagnosed with autism...(aged 33!).'
YouTube. Accessed on 13/9/2021 at https://www.youtube.com/
watch?v=YgxHpHIrGNY.

Yo Samdy Sam (2020) 'Autistic MASKING: How do we do it and should
we stop?' YouTube. Accessed on 13/9/2021 at www.youtube.com/
watch?v=t9COmZ2HwXY&t=356s.

Ben Coyle-Larner (aka Loyle Carner)

Aroesti, R. (2019) 'Loyle Carner: Not Waving, But Drowning review –
heartfelt hip-hop.' *The Guardian*, 19 April. Accessed on 13/9/2021 at
www.theguardian.com/music/2019/apr/19/loyle-carner-not-waving-
but-drowning-review.

Carner, L. (2020) 'I thought I was a crazy kid.' ADDitude, updated 14
December. Accessed on 13/9/2021 at www.additudemag.com/loyle-
carner-british-musician-on-adhd.

Cooper, L. (2017) 'Loyle Carner – "Yesterday's Gone" Review.' *NME*, 25
January. Accessed on 13/9/2021 at www.nme.com/reviews/loyle-
carner-yesterdays-gone-review-1959441.

Cumming, E. (2016) 'Rapper's delight: How musician Loyle Carner is teaching kids to cook.' *The Observer*, 21 August. Accessed on 13/9/2021 at www.theguardian.com/global/2016/aug/21/rappers-delight-how-musician-loyle-carner-is-teaching-kids-to-cook.

Lewis, T. (2019) 'Interview – Loyle Carner: "I was raised by women – they talked about feelings every day."' *The Observer*, 21 April. Accessed on 13/9/2021 at www.theguardian.com/music/2019/apr/21/loyle-carner-i-was-raised-by-women-talk-about-feelings-every-day-not-waving-but-drowning.

Mercury Prize (2012) 'Previous shortlists.' Accessed on 13/9/2021 at www.mercuryprize.com/previous%20shortlists.

O'Connor, R. (2017) 'Loyle Carner and Benjamin Zephaniah talk art, dyslexia and Shakespeare. Exclusive video: Mercury Prize-shortlisted artist spoke with the award-winning poet in a filmed conversation.' *The Independent*, 9 September. Accessed on 13/9/2021 at www.independent.co.uk/arts-entertainment/music/features/loyle-carner-benjamin-zephaniah-interview-mercury-prize-poetry-rap-hip-hop-video-watch-a7935786.html.

Piskorz, J. and Thompson, K. (2019) 'Watch Loyle Carner give ES Magazine an exclusive tour of his pop-up art gallery.' *Evening Standard*, 18 April. Accessed on 13/9/2021 at www.standard.co.uk/lifestyle/esmagazine/loyle-carner-es-magazine-art-exhibition-a4121491.html.

Smith, S. (2016) 'Not Waving but Drowning.' Poetry Foundation. Accessed on 13/9/2021 at www.poetryfoundation.org/poems/46479/not-waving-but-drowning.

Jonathon Drane (aka Jono Drane)

ADHD Foundation (n.d.) 'Patrons: Jonathan Drane.' Accessed on 13/9/2021 at https://adhdfoundation.org.uk/patron/jonathan-drane.

British Judo (2014) 'Jono Drane joins forces with ADHD Foundation.' GB Judo News, 21 July. Accessed on 13/9/2021 at www.britishjudo.org.uk/jono-drane-joins-forces-with-adhd-foundation/?doing_wp_cron=16303369 72.4113440513610839843750.

British Judo (2020) 'Rio Paralympian Jonathan Drane announces retirement.' Accessed on 13/9/2021 at www.britishjudo.org.uk/rio-paralympian-jonathan-drane-announces-retirement.

JudoInside.com (n.d.) 'Jonathan Drane judoka.' Accessed on 13/9/2021 at www.judoinside.com/judoka/49877/Jonathan_Drane/judo-career.

JudoInside.com (n.d.) 'Judo results: Jonathan Drane.' Accessed on 13/9/2021 at www.judoinside.com/judoka/49877/Jonathan_Drane/judo-results.

Mahmood, A. (2016) 'Paralympic judoka Jonathan Drane to retire – at the age of 29.' *Eastern Daily Press*, 10 October. Accessed on 13/9/2021 at www.edp24.co.uk/sport/paralympic-judoka-jonathan-drane-to-retire-at-the-age-of-939864.

TEDx Talks (2018) 'The Power of Trying | Jono Drane | TEDxNorwichED.' YouTube. Accessed on 13/9/2021 at www.youtube.com/watch?v=f_j4sOvDBfw.

Dara McAnulty

Hutton, A. (2020) 'Michael Gove didn't stay to listen but the Greta Thunberg of Northern Ireland wrote a book.' *The Times*, 1 March. Accessed on 13/9/2021 at www.thetimes.co.uk/article/michael-gove-didnt-stay-to-listen-but-the-greta-thunberg-of-northern-ireland-wrote-a-book-kzwhvkd3b.

McAnulty, D. (2016) 'My story so far. Autism and nature.' Accessed on 13/9/2021 athttps://daramcanulty.com/about.

McAnulty, D. (2016) 'Unlikely activist – Hen Harrier Day 2016.' Accessed on 13/9/2021 at https://daramcanulty.com/2016/08/06/unlikely-activist-hen-harrier-day-2016.

McAnulty, D. (2020) *Diary of a Young Naturalist*. Beaminster: Little Toller Books.

McAnulty, D. (2021) 'Dara McAnulty | RTÉ Home School Hub.' YouTube. Accessed on 13/9/2021 at www.youtube.com/watch?v=-Ac4ToafM1s.

Preston, A. (2020) 'Diary of a Young Naturalist by Dara McAnulty review – miraculous memoir.' *The Observer*, 7 June. Accessed on 13/9/2021 at www.theguardian.com/books/2020/jun/07/diary-of-a-young-naturalist-by-dara-mcanulty-review-miraculous-memoir.

Ryan Higa

Higa, R. and Nugroho, J. (2017) *Ryan Higa's How to Write Good*. London: Little, Brown Books For Young Readers.

nigahaga (n.d.) 'Off the Pill Podcast #1 – ADHD, brand deals, and choosing to be gay?' YouTube. Accessed on 13/9/2021 at www.youtube.com/watch?v=kpwPoIgkPK4&t=2512s.

nigahaga (2013) 'Draw my life – Ryan Higa.' YouTube. Accessed on 13/9/2021 at www.youtube.com/watch?v=KPmoDYayoLE&t=392s.

YouTube (n.d.) 'nigahiga' [YouTube channel]. www.youtube.com/c/ryanhiga/about. Accessed on 13/9/2021 at www.youtube.com/c/ryanhiga/about.

Temple Grandin

Dailymotion (n.d.) '[Documentary] Horizon 2006 The woman who thinks like a cow.' Accessed on 13/9/2021 at www.dailymotion.com/video/x6xhl12.

Demuth, P. and Squier, R. (2020) *Who Is Temple Grandin?* New York, NY: Penguin Workshop.

Grandin, T. (2021) Wired Differently research interview with Temple Grandin, 12 February.

Grandin, T. and Scariano, M. (2005) *Emergence: Labeled Autistic. A True Story*. New York, NY: Warner Books.

Jessica McCabe

Maguire, C. (2021) 'Hello, Brains! A life spent helping others understand A.D.H.D.' *The New York Times*, 22 February. Accessed on 13/9/2021 at www.nytimes.com/2021/02/22/style/self-care/adhd-youtube.html.

TEDx Talks (2017) 'Failing at normal: An ADHD success story | Jessica McCabe | TEDxBratislava.' Accessed on 13/9/2021 at YouTube. www.youtube.com/watch?v=JiwZQNYlGQI&t=344s.

YouTube (n.d.) 'How to ADHD.' [YouTube channel]. Accessed on 13/9/2021 at www.youtube.com/channel/UC-nPM1_kSZf91ZGkcgy_95Q.

Hannah Gadsby

Hannah Gadsby: Douglas (2020) [film]. Netflix.

Hannah Gadsby: Nanette (2018) [film]. Netflix.

TED (2019) 'Three ideas. Three contradictions. Or not. | Hannah Gadsby.' YouTube. Accessed on 13/9/2021 at www.youtube.com/watch?v=87qLWFZManA&t=915s.

The Companion to Tasmanian History (n.d.) 'Gay law reform.' Accessed on 13/9/2021 at www.utas.edu.au/library/companion_to_tasmanian_history/G/Gay%20Law%20Reform.htm.

Token (n.d.) 'Hannah Gadsby.' Accessed on 13/9/2021 at https://token.com.au/artist/hannah-gadsby.

Wright, T. (2017) 'Why Hannah Gadsby is retiring from comedy after "Nanette".' *The Sydney Morning Herald,* 30 June. Accessed on 13/9/2021 at www.smh.com.au/entertainment/comedy/why-hannah-gadsby-is-retiring-from-comedy-after-nanette-20170628-gxo313.html.

Stephen Wiltshire

shippy555 (2012) 'The foolish wise ones QED – 1986 Part 2 (of 2).' YouTube. Accessed on 13/9/2021 at www.youtube.com/watch?v=GX2k4whjsEM&t=611s.

Wiltshire, S. (n.d.) 'An artist was born.' Accessed on 13/9/2021 at www.stephenwiltshire.co.uk/biography.

Wiltshire, S. (1989) *Cities.* London: J.M. Dent & Sons.

Wiltshire, S. (1991) *Floating Cities: Venice, Amsterdam, Leningrad and Moscow.* London: Joseph.

Wiltshire, S. (2020) 'Billions of windows | Full Movie | HD | Genius Artist | Documentary | Drawings | 2021.' YouTube. Accessed on 13/9/2021 at www.youtube.com/watch?v=TOoGokjEri8&t=1369s.

Wiltshire, S. and Casson, H. (1987) Drawings. London: J.M. Dent & Sons.

Polly Samuel (aka Donna Williams)

Brenner, A. (2021) Wired Differently research interview with Andrew Brenner (friend of Polly Samuel), 17 June.

Polly's pages (aka 'Donna Williams') (2015) 'We're all multiple – Legion Theory and my DID team.' Accessed on 13/9/2021 at https://blog.donnawilliams.net/2015/04/22/7151.

Polly's pages (aka 'Donna Williams') (2015) 'What is a gadoodleborger?' Accessed on 13/9/2021 at https://blog.donnawilliams.net/2015/01/04/what-is-a-gadoodleborger.

Samuel, C. (2019) 'Vale Polly Samuel (1963–2017): On dying & death.' The musings of Chris Samuel, 22 April. Accessed on 13/9/2021 at www.csamuel.org/2019/04/22/on-dying-and-death.

Sinclair, J. (n.d.) 'Autism Network International: The development of a community and its culture.' Accessed on 13/9/2021 at www.autismnetworkinternational.org/History_of_ANI.html.

Sinclair, J. (n.d.) 'Don't mourn for us.' Accessed on 13/9/2021 at www.autreat.com/dont_mourn.html.

Williams, D. (n.d.) 'About diagnosis.' Accessed on 13/9/2021 at www.donnawilliams.net/indexf5b0.html?id=diagnosis.

Williams, D. (1992) *Nobody Nowhere*. London: Doubleday.

Williams, D. (1995) *Somebody Somewhere*. London: Corgi.

Ann Bancroft

Ann Bancroft Foundation (2018) 'About Ann Bancroft.' Accessed on 13/9/2021 at https://web.archive.org/web/20180415183909/http:/www.annbancroftfoundation.org/about-us/about-abf.

Ann Bancroft Foundation (2021) 'Our mission.' Accessed on 13/9/2021 at www.annbancroftfoundation.org/about/mission.

Arnesen, L., Bancroft, A. and Dahle, C. (2004) *No Horizon Is So Far: Two Women and Their Extraordinary Journey Across Antarctica*. Waterville, ME: Thorndike Press.

Forbes (2001) 'Because it's there.' Accessed on 13/9/2021 atwww.forbes.com/global/2001/1029/060.html?sh=22bfa7ca2080.

The Yale Center for Dyslexia & Creativity (n.d.) 'Ann Bancroft, polar explorer.' Accessed on 13/9/2021 at http://dyslexia.yale.edu/story/ann-bancroft.

Laura Kate Dale

Dale, L.K. (2019) *Uncomfortable Labels: My Life as a Gay Autistic Trans Woman*. London: Jessica Kingsley Publishers.

Dale, L.K. (2021) Wired Differently research interview with Laura Kate Dale, 23 February.

Dale, L.K. (ed.) (2021) *Gender Euphoria: Stories of Joy from Trans, Non-Binary and Intersex Writers*. London: Unbound.

Emma Lewell-Buck

BBC News (2013) 'Labour win South-Shields by-election.' Politics, 3 May. Accessed on 13/9/2021 at www.bbc.co.uk/news/av/world-us-canada-22393353.

BBC News (2013) 'South Shields by-election: Labour wins as UKIP makes big gains.' Politics, 3 May Accessed on 13/9/2021 at www.bbc.co.uk/news/uk-politics-22393094.

ITV News (2019) 'Emma Lewell-Buck on accents, dyspraxia and siding with the Brexit Party over the Lib Dems | ITV News.' YouTube. Accessed on 13/9/2021 at www.youtube.com/watch?v=ygoUxzos56c&t=393s.

Pring, J. (2019) 'MP speaks of pride at being dyspraxic at launch of Neurodivergent Labour.' Disability News Service, 14 February. Accessed on 13/9/2021 at www.disabilitynewsservice.com/mp-speaks-of-pride-at-being-dyspraxic-at-launch-of-neurodivergent-labour.

Reynolds, D. (2020) 'Jessica Benham, bi autistic woman, seals historic win in pa. election.' Advocate, 6 November. Accessed on 13/9/2021 at www.advocate.com/election/2020/11/06/jessica-benham-bi-autistic-woman-seals-historic-win-pa-election.

Rowley, T. (2013) 'I'd love to wear eyeliner, but that requires a steady hand.' *The Telegraph*, 28 September. Accessed on 13/9/2021 at www.telegraph.co.uk/women/womens-life/10341479/Id-love-to-wear-eyeliner-but-that-requires-a-steady-hand.html.

UK Parliament (2015) '2015 General election results: South Shields.' Accessed on 13/9/2021 at https://electionresults.parliament.uk/election/2015-05-07/Results/Location/Constituency/South%20Shields.

UK Parliament (2017) '2017 General election results: South Shields.'

Accessed on 13/9/2021 at https://electionresults.parliament.uk/
election/2017-06-08/Results/Location/Constituency/South%20Shields.

Elle McNicoll

Big DoG (2020) 'Elle McNicoll – diversity in publishing.' YouTube. Accessed
on 13/9/2021 at www.youtube.com/watch?v=eBJ91G550cY&t=949s.

Blue Peter (2021) 'Blue Peter Book Awards 2021 WINNERS!'
YouTube. Accessed on 13/9/2021 athttps://www.youtube.com/
watch?v=LhnMKwGGpYo.

ellemcnicoll.com (2018) 'About Elle.' Accessed on 13/9/2021 at https://
ellemcnicoll.com.

Knights Of (n.d.) '#Books Made Better.' Accessed on 13/9/2021 at http://
knightsof.media.

McNicoll, E. (2020) *A Kind of Spark*. London: Knights Of.

McNicoll, E. (2021) *Show Us Who You Are*. London: Knights Of.

Sam Holness (aka Super Sam)

Holness, S. and Holness, A. (2021) Wired Differently research interview with
Sam Holness, 19 March.

Run247 (2021) 'HOKA ONE ONE Announces Sam Holness as global athlete
ambassador.' News, 5 January. Accessed on 13/9/2021 at https://run247.
com/running-news/hoka-one-one-announces-sam-holness-as-
global-athlete-ambassador.

Shaw Trust Disability Power 100 List (n.d.) 'Sam Holness.' Accessed on
13/9/2021 at https://disabilitypower100.com/project/sam-holness

UKRunChat (2021) 'Super Sam Holness and Tony Holness.'
Accessed on 13/9/2021 at www.instagram.com/tv/CMMnHfkh_
fe/?igshid=1khy7ob5ub9sg.

Mickey Rowe

Academy of Motion Picture Arts and Sciences. (n.d.) 'The 61st Academy

Awards | 1989.' Accessed on 13/9/2021 at www.oscars.org/oscars/ceremonies/1989/R?qt-honorees=1#block-quicktabs-honorees.

Andreeva, N. (2020) '"Atypical" renewed for fourth & final season by Netflix.' Deadline, 24 February. Accessed on 13/9/2021 at https://deadline.com/2020/02/atypical-renewed-season-4-final-season-netflix-premiere-date-2021-1202866580.

Collins-Hughes, L. (2017) 'The world really is a stage, scripts and all, to an actor with autism.' The New York Times, 6 November. Accessed on 13/9/2021 at www.nytimes.com/2017/11/06/theater/actor-with-autism-curious-incident-of-the-dog-in-the-night-time.html.

CNN (n.d.) 'Actor with autism takes centre stage.' Accessed on 13/9/2021 at https://edition.cnn.com/videos/tv/2017/10/29/gbs-autistic-actor.great-big-story.

Fierberg, R. (2017) 'First production of Curious Incident starring an actor with autism begins September 19.' Playbill, 19 September. Accessed on 13/9/2021 at www.playbill.com/article/the-first-production-of-curious-incident-starring-an-actor-with-autism-begins-tonight.

Huffpost (2019) 'Why autistic actors should be cast in more roles | Mickey Rowe.' YouTube. Accessed on 13/9/2021 at www.youtube.com/watch?v=Jmj9c825Nss.

National Disability Theatre (n.d.) 'Mission.' Accessed on 13/9/2021 at https://nationaldisabilitytheatre.org/mission-1.

Parrotta, M. (2018) 'An introduction to the National Disability Theatre: In conversation with Mickey Rowe.' The Theatre Times, 23 December. Accessed on 13/9/2021 at https://thetheatretimes.com/an-introduction-to-the-national-disability-theatre-in-conversation-with-mickey-rowe.

Richardson, J. (2021) 'Ashley Storrie starring in BBC autism comedy dinosaur.' [online] British Comedy Guide, 8 March. Accessed on 13/9/2021 at www.comedy.co.uk/online/news/6242/dinosaur-ashley-storrie.

Rowe, M. (2015) 'Our differences are our strengths: Neurodiversity in theatre.' HowlRound Theatre Commons. Accessed on 13/9/2021 at https://howlround.com/our-differences-are-our-strengths.

Rowe, M. (2020) 'Yes, we can act: A professional autistic actor's response to Sia.' The Mighty, 25 November. Accessed on 13/9/2021 at https://themighty.com/2020/11/actor-mickey-rowe-sia-music-autism.

Rozsa, M. (2017) 'For once, an autistic role will be played by an autistic actor.' Salon, 15 May. Accessed on 13/9/2021 at www.salon.com/2017/05/15/mickey-rowe-the-curious-incident-of-the-dog-at-night-time-autistic.

Siena Castellon

Castellon, S. (2020) The Spectrum Girl's Survival Guide: How to Grow Up Awesome and Autistic. London: Jessica Kingsley Publishers.

GMB Union (2021) 'Neurodiversity Celebration Week 2021.' Accessed on 13/9/2021 at www.gmb.org.uk/long-read/neurodiversity-celebration-week-2021.

Quantum Leap Mentoring (n.d.) 'What to do if you are being bullied.' Accessed on 13/9/2021 at www.qlmentoring.com/what-to-do-if-you-are-being-bullied.

Teen Hero Awards 2018 (2018) 'Teen Hero Awards 2018 – Siena's story.' YouTube. Accessed on 13/9/2021 at www.youtube.com/watch?v=A3KZFvgUV8s.

The Different Minds Podcast Series (2020) 'Neurodiversity – the new normal' [podcast]. Accessed on 13/9/2021 at https://open.spotify.com/episode/4pqqfJ755MaYUQRZltVPaH?si=M6W3L5WHTpeSxi-F38be2g&dl_branch=1.

United Nations Office of the Secretary-General's Envoy on Youth (n.d.) 'Siena Castellon.' Accessed on 13/9/2021 at www.un.org/youthenvoy/siena-castellon.

Suzi Ruffell

Foundry Fox (2018) 'We catch up with London funny-girl Suzi Ruffell.' Accessed on 13/9/2021 at www.foundryfox.com/5671/funny-girl-suzi-ruffell/#.4MFaiMbyq6.

Ruffell, S. (2017). '"Slagging a skanky gaff": Suzi Ruffell's unforgettable five gigs.' Chortle. Accessed on 13/9/2021 at www.chortle.co.uk/unforgettablefive/2017/01/27/26731/slagging_a_skanky_gaff.

Ruffell, S. (2018) 'A new start: Suzi Ruffell on growing up dyslexic and discovering the joy of writing.' *The Guardian*, 30 December. Accessed on 13/9/2021 at www.theguardian.com/lifeandstyle/2018/dec/30/a-new-start-suzi-ruffell-on-growing-up-dyslexic-and-discovering-the-joy-of-writing.

Ruffell, S. (2021) Wired Differently research interview with Suzi Ruffell, 22 January.

Jon Adams

Adams, J. (2020) Wired Differently research interview with Jon Adams, 15 December.

Learn From Autistics (2019) 'Autism Interview #113: Jon Adams on autism, art, and the Flow Observatorium.' Accessed on 13/9/2021 at www.learnfromautistics.com/autism-interview-113-jon-adams-on-autism-art-and-the-flow-observatorium.

Nitter by PussTheCat.org (n.d.) 'Autism care and share (@autcareandshare).' Accessed on 13/9/2021 at https://nitter.pussthecat.org/autcareandshare/status/1428247380084862976.

Simone Biles

Biles, S. (2018) *Courage to Soar: A Body in Motion, A Life in Balance*. Grand Rapids, MI: Zondervan.

Kumar, A. (2021) 'Simone Biles discusses her mental health, challenges after winning bronze on beam.' ESPN.com. Accessed on 13/9/2021 at www.espn.co.uk/olympics/story/_/id/31953744/olympics-2021-simone-biles-explains-challenges-balance-beam-final.

mid-day.com (2017) 'ADHD is not a disability, it's a super power: Simone Biles.' Accessed on 8/10/2021 at www.mid-day.com/sports/other-sports/article/ADHD-is-not-a-disability--it-s-a-super-power--Simone-Biles-18657172.

Morgan, S.J. (2020) *Simone Biles*. London: Stripes Publishing.

The Athletic (2021) '2021 Olympics: Simone Biles wins bronze medal with gutsy performance on beam.' Accessed on 13/9/2021 at https://

theathletic.com/news/2021-olympics-simone-biles-wins-bronze-
medal-with-gutsy-performance-on-beam/owUVIxBZtSjm.

Goodbye

BBC News Finland (2015) 'Finland punk band PKN set for Eurovision.'
Entertainment and Arts, 1 March. Accessed on 13/9/2021 at www.bbc.
co.uk/news/entertainment-arts-31682196.

Silberman, S. (2016) *NeuroTribes: The Legacy of Autism and the Future of
Neurodiversity*. New York, NY: Penguin Random House.

Tiergarten Records (n.d.) 'About.' Accessed on 13/9/2021 at www.
tiergartenrecords.com/about.

University of Michigan Dyslexia Help (n.d.) 'Muhammad Ali.' Accessed
on 13/9/2021 at http://dyslexiahelp.umich.edu/success-stories/
muhammad-ali#:~:text=Ali%20was%20diagnosed%20with%20dyslexia.

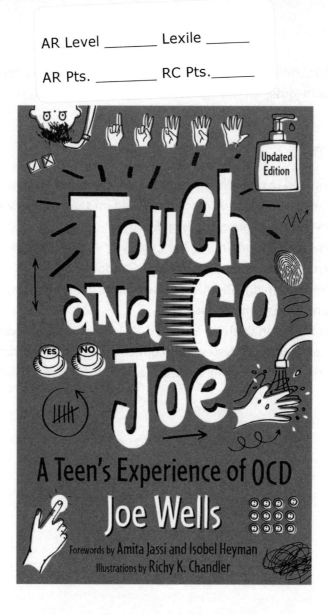

Touch and Go Joe, Updated Edition

A Teen's Experience of OCD

Joe Wells

Forewords by Amita Jassi and Isobel Heyman

Illustrations by Richy K. Chandler

ISBN 978 1 78775 777 6

eISBN 978 1 78775 778 3